"To motivate salespeople, you must be able to truly understand what makes them tick and what they are passionate about! It takes some managers years to learn this skill. Read *Selling Is Everyone's Business* and you will become a master motivator of your sales team a heck of a lot faster."

—Greg Stubblefield, President of California
and Hawaii Area, Enterprise Rent-A-Car

"Is selling really everyone's business? When you consider what would happen without the efforts of the men and women who keep the money flowing in, you've got to admit the answer is yes. Johnson and Shaivitz have written an outstanding guide to motivating these key players and helping them excel beyond their (and your) wildest dreams."

—Managing Director
at a Leading Global Private Bank

SELLING
IS EVERYONE'S
BUSINESS

SELLING
IS EVERYONE'S
BUSINESS

WHAT IT TAKES TO CREATE
A GREAT SALESPERSON

Steve Johnson & Adam Shaivitz

WILEY

John Wiley & Sons, Inc.

Published by John Wiley & Sons, Inc., Hoboken, New Jersey.
Published simultaneously in Canada.

For general information on our other products and services or for technical support, please contact our Customer Care Department within the United States at (800) 762-2974, outside the United States at (317) 572-3993 or fax (317) 572-4002.

Wiley also publishes its books in a variety of electronic formats. Some content that appears in print may not be available in electronic books. For more information about Wiley products, visit our web site at www.wiley.com.

Library of Congress Cataloging-in-Publication Data:

Johnson, Steve, 1962–
    Selling is everyone's business : what it takes to create a great salesperson / Steve Johnson, Adam Shaivitz.
       p. cm.
    Includes index.
    ISBN-13: 978-0-471-77673-4 (cloth)
    ISBN-10: 0-471-77673-4 (cloth)
    1. Sales personnel—Training of.   2. Selling.   I. Shaivitz, Adam, 1976–
II. Title.
HF5439.8.J65   2006
658.8'1—dc22

                                          2005031913

Printed in the United States of America.

10 9 8 7 6 5 4 3 2 1

Contents

Acknowledgments

We have been so fortunate to have coaches, mentors, and friends there to support us before, during, and after the creation of this book.

To our colleagues: Bob Coakley, Chad Carden, Mark Norman, Nate Brooks, Bob Davis, and Jack Litzelfelner—thank you. We have a great respect for each of you.

Thanks to Dawn Mitchell and Donene Kistler for all your help every day around the office.

Thank you to Celia Rocks, Dottie DeHart, and the people at Rocks-DeHart Public Relations.

Thank you to Larry Alexander, Matt Holt, Shannon Vargo, Kate Lindsay, and the team at John Wiley & Sons for all of your guidance and feedback.

Thanks to all of the clients of The Next Level. If it were not for you, we would not be where we are today. We have the best clients that a business could ever be blessed with.

(SRJ) Thanks to my wife Elisa, who has been an absolute rock to me for the eight years that we have been married.

Thanks to the two most special children in the world, Matthew and Anna, who are a constant reminder to me of what life is really about.

Thanks to my parents, Al and Donna Johnson, who are about the finest role models that a son could ever have.

Thanks to Adam Shaivitz for his tenacity and his partnership in getting this book done.

(AHS) Dave Baiada, Howie Blank, Dorothy D. Choi, Brian Goldberg, Scott and Craig Hochstadt, Nitya Kirat, Jamie McIntosh, Brian Naftaly, Kevin Pryse, Matt Salganik, Bobby Sanchez, Keith Schultz, Mel Williams, Bryan Wollheim, and Mo Zahrawi—thanks for always being there with encouragement and a sense of humor.

Thank you to Steve Johnson for working together with me on this project and for giving me every opportunity to succeed in our business.

Thank you to Grandma Bernice and Grandma Blanche for always being my biggest fans, regardless of what I do.

Thank you to Melissa Felton, the finest biscuit in all of the land, for your relentless optimism and consistent late-night phone calls of encouragement.

Thank you to Jeff for helping me see the lighter side of everything I've ever taken too seriously.

Thank you to Mom and Dad—you are easily the best two life coaches a guy could ever ask for.

Introduction

The score is tied in the fourth quarter of a classic college football game when a coach comes upon a challenging situation. It's the biggest game of the season against his team's hugest rival (comparable to an Ohio State–Michigan rivalry). The game is in early December and the field is covered with snow. The team's starting quarterback hurt his ankle in practice on Thursday before the big game. The second-string quarterback goes down with a shoulder injury early in the fourth quarter, and the team is backed up inside its own 10-yard line. The coach walks down the sideline to the third-string quarterback, a freshman who has not taken a snap all season and is shivering from the cold. The coach gives him very specific directions: "We need you, son. Here's what you're gonna do. You're going to run the ball for three plays, and on the fourth play, you're gonna punt." The quarterback nods his head and jogs slowly into the huddle. On the first play, he hands the ball off to the running back, who runs around the right end for a gain of 20 yards. On the next play, he hands the ball off to the running back, who runs around the left end for a gain of 30 yards. On the next play he hands the ball off again to the running back, who runs straight up the middle for a gain of 40 yards. At this point, the ball is inside the opponent's 10-yard line. On the fourth play, before the center snaps the ball, the quarterback drops back into punt formation. He receives the long snap and proceeds to punt the ball out of the stadium. When he jogs over to the sideline, the coach is waiting for him. The coach grabs the quarterback by the shoulder pads and screams: "Son! What on earth were you thinking out there?" To which the quarterback replies: "I was thinking that I must have the dumbest coach in the world!"

In this example, the coach was not particularly effective. We do, however, believe that coaching does work very well when it is executed properly, which is what this book is all about. In fact, we believe coaching is a key cog in the creation of a great salesperson. So if you coach others, have a coach, or coach yourself, you have the right book in your hands!

Why Did We Write This Book?

Selling is everyone's business. You are in sales if your job is to move a product, service, or concept, tangible or intangible, whether you work in inside sales or outside sales in a territory, and whether you work over the phone or face-to-face. If you are not a salesperson by trade, you are still selling something if you have ever tried to convince a friend or your spouse to see a certain movie or eat at a certain restaurant, if you have ever tried to show your child the benefit of doing homework, if you have ever tried to sell an idea to coworkers, if you have ever tried to get someone to invest in your idea, or if you ever had to fight the battle of mind over mattress to sell yourself on the idea of getting out of bed early to work out. Everyone needs to develop an ability to sell.

We bring you: *What It Takes to Create a Great Salesperson.* While a small minority of people are able to build this ideal salesperson in themselves, we believe the majority of us benefit significantly from some form of sales coach. Either way, this text will serve as a toolkit to help you create a great salesperson in yourself if you are a salesperson, or within your sales team if you are a coach.

We have used the term *great* several times already to describe the salesperson that this book will help you to create or become. A *great* salesperson will have different characteristics that can vary somewhat based on the type of sales organization in which the salesperson operates. The following are a few examples that we use to define greatness in a salesperson.

- A great salesperson exceeds sales goals, every time, in every period, with no excuses.
- A great salesperson is looked up to as a role model by others on the sales team and throughout the organization.
- A great salesperson represents the company in a way that supports the firm's overall strategy.
- A great salesperson finds unique ways to improve himself and his team.
- A great salesperson has a relentless attitude toward self-improvement.

Again, these are just examples of traits that help define greatness in sales based on what we have observed in top performers. Anyone who has been a professional salesperson knows that achieving such greatness is not easy.

This book takes into consideration the numerous factors and associated challenges facing the workforce today.

- With Generation Y (18–22), Generation X (23–37), Baby Boomers (38–57), and Matures (58+) all in the workplace, the workforce is more dynamic and diverse than ever before. Today's successful coach and salesperson must be able to adapt to different people with different sets of priorities.
- Today there are more technologies and means of communication than ever before. While this creates great opportunity for sales professionals, it also creates challenges. It is not always easy to communicate with a salesperson or a coach using the ideal means of communication. Sometimes people will use e-mail or voice mail to communicate messages that should ideally be delivered face-to-face.
- Competition in almost every industry continues to increase. Accordingly, sales professionals are challenged to do more with less, get more out of existing customers, and find creative ways to generate more business.

We have seen many sales coaches and salespeople struggle with these changes and challenges while others employ best practices that have enabled them to lead themselves or their teams to success. Whether you are a sales coach, you have a sales coach, or you are your own sales coach, this book outlines real top performer best sales coaching practices in an attempt to transfer them to you.

Who's the Book For?

"We could all use a little coaching. When you're playing the game, it's hard to think of everything."

—Jim Rohn, speaker and author

This book is appropriate for any person involved in a sales organization. It is especially relevant for anyone who must achieve results through the performance of others. Specifically, this book is for you if you are:

- **Someone who wants to start a career in sales.** Since working in sales is a great opportunity to control your own destiny, thousands enter the profession each year.
- **An entrepreneur, business owner, or independent salesperson.** You will learn how to set up accountability standards for yourself and be able to benchmark yourself against some of the best in the world.
- **A salesperson.** You can bring the ideas in this book to your company, or implement the management techniques to self-manage and improve your own performance.
- **A sales coach.** You have a team of salespeople and are constantly looking to improve your team's results.
- **A sales executive.** You oversee sales coaches who run teams of salespeople, so you are on the lookout for top practices that can improve your organization.

Who Are We?

We are principals in *The Next Level Sales Consulting*, a sales training and consulting company that works with clients within their sales and service organizations. Over the last several years, we have interacted with thousands of sales teams and sales coaches. From our time spent with these clients, we have amassed a vast collection of compelling stories and examples of what to do and what not to do as a sales coach. We have come to realize that our clients and the marketplace demand a "how-to" sales coaching tool based on best practices. Organizations know that the quickest way to improve their salespeople is to improve their sales coaches, because coaches have the most leverage. When a sales coach improves, her salespeople improve. The challenge is that, for most people, coaching is a vague, intangible, and nebulous concept. As with other complicated topics, there's a lot of theory out there but few proven effective best practices. This book makes coaching specific and tangible and puts it into a simple format that can be most easily executed.

Sales and sales coaching are two functions in which "street cred," or street credibility, is extremely valuable. This is because top performing salespeople and sales coaches typically make more money than mediocre performers, so people are interested in learning and emulating what the top producers are doing. This book is based on the findings of the principals of The Next Level Sales Consulting, all of whom have significant sales and sales coaching experience, including:

- A salesperson who performed in the top 1 percent in a worldwide sales training organization with over 1,000 salespeople.
- A salesperson who quickly rose through the ranks in sales and sales coaching in the travel industry.
- A salesperson who has been a top performer in sales, sales coaching, and marketing positions in the education and pharmaceutical industries.
- A salesperson who has been a high achiever in the sales training field and as an entrepreneur.

Currently, at The Next Level, we work with numerous high-profile clients and smaller organizations, including Automatic Data Processing (ADP), A.G. Edwards & Sons, Inc., Adelphia, Countrywide Financial Corp., Enterprise Rent-A-Car, The Los Angeles Clippers, Maly's, Morgan Stanley, Piper Jaffray, RBC Dain Rauscher, UBS Financial Services, and Vanguard (Alamo and National Car Rental). For these wide-ranging clients we perform a variety of functions including determining best practices, designing sales/service improvement programs, facilitating instructor-led training, implementing follow-up plans with sales executives and sales coaches, keeping score of results to track a return on investment, and delivering keynote speeches.

Through this experience, The Next Level has worked with more than 500,000 salespeople and more than 10,000 sales coaches and sales executives over 50 combined years. So it's important to recognize that not all of the ideas in this book are ours. We have been fortunate enough to meet thousands of talented performers and observe some tremendous best practices in our clients, and now we are in a qualified position to share them.

What's in the Book?

This book will be practical, yet fun to read. It is filled with real quotes, examples, and success stories from our clients and from our own experiences in sales and sales coaching over the years. We feel pretty lucky because, at The Next Level, it is our job to interact with people doing sales coaching every day. We also feel fortunate for you, our reader. If you are involved in a sales organization or if you are an entrepreneur (whom many would consider to be the ultimate salesperson), you will find this material extremely relevant and executable.

One quick note regarding the content: most chapters are primarily focused on how to become a great sales coach who builds great salespeople and sales teams. Many chapters also include segments that approach the same chapter topic from the perspective of both the sales coach and the salesperson.

What are the Benefits of Reading this Book?

(AHS) Several months before starting to write this book I was having dinner with my paternal grandmother. She asked me about work and what was new for me, so I mentioned that I had an exciting opportunity coming up to write a book. The conversation went something like this:

> *Adam:* I'm writing a book later this summer. It should be an interesting experience.
> *Grandma Blanche:* Really. What is the book about?
> *Adam:* Sales coaching. I think I can get you a pretty good deal on a copy. Will you read it?
> *Grandma Blanche:* Adam, I love you very much, and I love to read. But I see absolutely no benefit to me in reading that book.

Clearly, my grandmother is a "tell it like it is" kind of woman, which I appreciate. After the conversation, I thanked Grandma Blanche for the friendly reminder that I should highlight the benefits of the book to readers as they are getting started. Fortunately for me, I have another grandmother. When a similar topic came up in a conversation between me and my maternal Grandma Bernice, I was more prepared and ready to present some benefits:

Adam: Grandma, I'm writing a book and I'm pretty excited about it!

Grandma Bernice: Really, that's nice.

Adam: It will be great for you when I get you a copy because you'll be able to read it and you'll also be able to show it off to your friends and brag about me.

Grandma Bernice: My friends already know how great you are. But maybe if I read that book, I'll actually be able to understand what you do for a living?

I presented benefits to Grandma Bernice, and she realized even more potential benefits on her own. It's been said that the most popular radio station in everyone's car is WIIFM—What's In It For Me? Like my grandmothers, you'll be giving up some of your valuable time to read this book, and you are asking yourself: "Is this going to be worth it?" Interestingly, as I sit here writing it, I'm wondering: "Is it worth my time to write the thing?" What follows are several of the benefits you can take away from your investment in reading this book. Keep in mind that these should be applicable to you whether you are new to sales, an entrepreneur, a salesperson, a sales coach, or a sales executive. In this book, you will learn:

- To take your individual or your team's performance to the next level.
- The role of the coach.
- To develop a coaching game plan for yourself or your team.

- To execute the game plan and be able to interact with our organization in the process.

- To convert C players to B players or move C players out of the organization, B players to A players, and A players to future company leaders.

- To implement the best practices used by top sales managers who lead teams at some of the world's top sales organizations.

- To develop a systematic approach to executing a business plan for yourself or a team member.

- To increase sales activity and effectiveness for yourself or your team.

- To give feedback that motivates and inspires your team regardless of their current performance.

- To transfer the skills and best practices of top performers to everyone else on your sales team through training.

- To create an environment within your sales team that recognizes top performance and discourages mediocrity.

- To employ methods to bring you more success and make your professional and personal life more fun.

- To become an even more successful person, with regard to likeability, reputation, and income.

Get Ready!

"It is what you learn after you know it all that counts."
                —John Wooden, former UCLA basketball
                    coach who led his teams to an unprecedented
                    ten national championships

Most successful people in sales are pretty confident. If you are like most salespeople (and like us incidentally), you think you know it all. Fortunately, we have John Wooden (who many consider to be one of the greatest coaches ever) to keep us grounded. To gain from reading this book, you must consider the three A's: Attitude, Adapt, and Action. If you approach the concepts in this book with the outlook of "That idea doesn't really apply to me or my sales organization," you're probably correct. On the other hand, if you take a positive and open-minded *attitude*, you will approach new concepts by asking the question, "How can I take that concept and *adapt* it so that it is relevant to my particular situation?" Lastly, you can read all the books on earth, but you will not change results until you change your behavior with *action*. You must actually use the ideas in this book to create change. Realistically, if you take one or two good ideas from this investment of your time, we are confident you and your teammates will become significantly more successful.

If you have a sincere desire to be great, we suggest you continue reading. Otherwise, the book makes a fine doorstop.

1

Sales Coaching

"It is one of the most beautiful compensations of this life that no one can sincerely try to help another without helping themselves."

—Ralph Waldo Emerson

You have the right attitude, you are ready to learn, and you look forward to taking action on your new findings to create a great salesperson in yourself or your sales team. So far, so good. To understand sales coaching one should first understand the overall impact of coaching and recognize the differences between a coach and a traditional manager or boss. There are both benefits and obstacles to being a sales coach rather than a sales manager. At the end of this chapter, you will have the opportunity to take an assessment quiz and rank yourself or your coach against some of the top sales coaching best practices.

The Impact of Coaching

According to studies conducted by Tony Rutigliano (currently Vice President and Chief Learning Officer at Automatic Data Processing) and Benson Smith of The Gallup Organization, top quartile sales coaches (based on the scores of an employee-attitude assessment of the coaches' employees) had overall 56 percent higher customer loyalty, 38 percent higher productivity, 27 percent higher return on investment in sales, and 50 percent lower employee turnover than other managers. These results indicate that there is a direct correlation between being a strong coach or having strong coaches on your team and customer loyalty, productivity, return on investment, and employee retention.

Whether you are a seasoned veteran or a green bean, as coach or salesperson, you can benefit from stronger coaching. Michael Jordan, Mary Lou Retton, Tiger Woods, and Lance Armstrong have all been successful under great coaches—so has the four-year-old learning to ice skate or hit a ball off a tee.

Think of a person who has had a significant positive impact on your life or career. It may have been a drama coach, baseball coach, high school teacher, family member, friend, or boss. What type of impact did he or she have on you? How did that affect the quality of your personal or professional life? At the time that he or she was impacting you, did you realize it? We all have people who affect us significantly, and we often don't realize it until years later. The type of coach we will be describing and creating in this book is the man or woman who has a lasting impact on the sales team and is a huge contributor to the team's success.

(SRJ) I remember my first day in sales. My coach sat me down at a desk, and the first thing he said was that when I come to work I have to be true to myself—I work for myself. Between 8:00 A.M. and 5:00 P.M. I do not go to the dry cleaners or get my hair cut or go to the movies or happy hour. I must remain true to myself, he said. I need to talk to 50 people per day. Then he gave me a list of prospects to call, plus a script of what to say, and we role-played and practiced the script together until it was second nature to me. Then I started making calls. Periodically through the day he'd drop by and ask, "How's it going?" I would share with him the objections I received, and we would create responses and practice those. Then I'd make more calls. The entire first week was like this. Then we moved on every week to new skills, like how to make an outside face-to-face call or how to deliver a group presentation. Ten years, 120,000 cold calls, 5,000 face-to-face calls, and 1,500 group presentations later, I was one of the top ten out of over 1,000 salespeople in my company. I didn't comprehend it right away, but now as I look back at the coaching he gave me and the impact it had on my life, I realize he was extremely instrumental in my success.

Coaches can leave lasting impressions. We hope they will be positive ones.

Boss vs. Coach

Dog Named Salesman

Two men went duck hunting together every year for several years. They did not have a dog of their own so they went to the same lodge each year to rent a dog. Each time they rented the same retriever from the man who owned the lodge. The dog's name was Salesman, and they used him for a few years because Salesman gave them particularly good results. Then one year, they went back and Salesman wasn't available. "Salesman has been promoted to Boss," the owner told them. "Now all he does is sit around the office and bark at everyone!"

Many people have had the experience of working under a boss or manager who shouts orders. In a professional setting, people often think of superiors as people who tell them to do things. We have found that the most effective leaders in top organizations perceive their role as that of a coach, not a boss. That's why in this book we use the term coach where many would substitute boss or manager.

Some of the key differences between a boss and a coach are specified in the following list. In which category does your management style put you?

- A boss drives his people; a coach leads them.
- A boss depends on authority; a coach on goodwill.
- A boss inspires fear; a coach inspires enthusiasm.
- A boss says "I"; a coach says "We."
- A boss says "get here on time"; a coach gets there ahead of time.
- A boss fixes blame for the breakdown; a coach fixes the breakdown.
- A boss knows how it is done; a coach shows how.
- A boss says "go"; a coach says "Let's go."
- A boss uses people; a coach develops them.
- A boss sees today; a coach also looks at tomorrow.
- A boss commands; a coach asks.
- A boss never has enough time; a coach makes time for things that count.

- A boss is concerned with things; a coach is concerned with people.
- A boss lets his people know where he stands; a coach lets his people know where they stand.
- A boss works hard to produce; a coach works hard to help his people produce.
- A boss takes the credit; a coach gives it.

Clearly, the coach is more effective in building a great salesperson and leading a team to a collective goal. Helping people to become a great sales coach is the motivation behind writing this book.

What is a coach? *Roget's Thesaurus* lists *trainer, athletic director, tutor, private teacher*, and *mentor* as synonyms for the noun, coach. *Train, instruct, tutor, teach, drill, advise, guide*, and *direct* are all synonyms for the verb, to coach. Our definition of a *sales coach* is an individual who demonstrates skill, habits, and attitudes in a way that positively impacts the results of salespeople and/or a sales team. The activities that this person executes include planning, conducting one-on-one goal setting meetings, leading teaching and training sessions, following up, doing the job with the team members (coaching in the crunch), leading team meetings, giving advice, and providing recognition. Successful coaching is the act of doing all these things well enough to create great salespeople and a successful sales team.

As we work on the formula to create a great salesperson, we will follow the path, one step at a time, in the coaching model shown in Figure 1.1. We will discuss one piece of the framework in each chapter in this book.

Every piece of the model simply highlights another means for the coach to communicate with salespeople in a way that inspires

FIGURE 1.1   Coaching Model 01

great performance, which translates to the ultimate goal of success for everyone on the team. Each unit of this model represents an opportunity for a coach to help a salesperson become closer to greatness. The best sales coaches follow this model and effectively use each of its elements in conjunction with all the others to communicate a consistent message and drive salesperson development and achievement. Jill Lane, a Group Vice President at Enterprise Rent-A-Car, explains the value in having a clear sales coaching model: "Our leaders manage a variety of functions, not just sales. So having a structure of accountability around sales management enables us to keep sales management and sales growth as a priority."

Why Coach Your Salespeople?

Robert Ripley, in his famous column, *Believe It Or Not*, once said, "A plain bar of iron is worth $5. The same bar of iron, when made into horseshoes, is worth $10.50. If made into needles, it is worth $355. If made into penknife blades, it is worth $3,285, and if turned into balance springs for watches, that identical bar of iron becomes worth $300,000."

Here Ripley makes the point that there is often more potential opportunity than many of us realize initially. This is especially the case with people. Great coaches love the challenge of helping each team member reach his or her own potential. Whether you are trying to make yourself better with self-coaching or improve a team of people as their coach, it's important to consider the benefits that both the coach and the sales team achieve from coaching. The following list enumerates these benefits.

- Salespeople improve when sales coaches improve. As you become a better coach, you will improve the performance of your people.
- Coaching is meaningful. As Thomas Jefferson said, "Far and away the best prize that life offers is the chance to work hard at something worth doing."
- You have skills and knowledge that you can impart to others. Transferring these skills is a rewarding experience for you and your people.
- When you are a coach, you increase job retention of the right people.
- When you are a coach, you weed out the wrong people quickly, which is a benefit to you, your organization, and those people that get weeded out.
- Making your people better than they would be if they did not have a sales coach is rewarding.
- Over time, your company's profits will undoubtedly increase.
- You will be building a bench of future leaders within your team.

By the way, to be a great coach, you have to want to be a coach and want to help people and your organization grow. Otherwise, it's going to be hard to get excited about what this book will teach you. As Eddie Robinson, the former football coach at Grambling State University, who accumulated more wins than any other coach in NCAA history, puts it: "Coaching is a profession of love. You can't coach people unless you love them."

Why Sales Coaching Often Doesn't Happen

We recently observed one of our clients in a one-on-one "coaching" session with one of her salespeople. This particular coach is extremely intense and motivated by strong performances, and she really strives to have her people succeed. She successfully planned the meeting by setting a direction and goal for it: She wanted the salesperson to understand how important it was for him to make more appointments with prospects each week. When it came time to discuss sales activity, the coach's approach went like this: "You need to set more appointments each week. I want to see more appointments out of you! Go out and set some more [expletive] appointments!" She emphasized her commitment to her message by fiercely karate-chopping the table as she spoke. One thing the coach did well is that she was extremely consistent and clear with her message. (As consultants, we are trained to find the positive in every situation.) However, although the salesperson heard the message, he was not especially motivated when he left the meeting.

In this instance, there was an attempt at coaching but it did not really occur in a positive fashion. Sometimes coaching is happening; it is just not leading to the desired result. More often, we find that coaching is being entirely avoided. Avoidance behavior, the most sinister force in business, is when coaches find excuses not to spend time coaching their people. Pat Riley, four-time NBA Champion Coach and three-time NBA Coach of the Year, once observed, "There's no such thing as coulda, shoulda, and woulda. If you coulda and you shoulda, you woulda."

Here are several reasons why coaching does not happen in every sales team:

- The person in charge does not see the value in coaching. Many managers think their salespeople are going to sink or swim regardless of what other people around them do or do not do.
- Many people do not know how to coach a team of salespeople or have never had a great coach to learn from, which is why this book is here.
- Coaching is not easy; it is frustrating. It is difficult enough to change your own habits, let alone someone else's.
- Some people are challenging to work with. Superiors often shy away from coaching individuals they do not get along with easily.
- It can be daunting to implement coaching as a priority in your workday because it is not an activity that most people plan in their already overwhelming schedules.
- It is difficult to measure the results of coaching, since the changes that result often take time.
- Many people in charge of sales teams are promoted to managers because they were great salespeople, not great coaches (like the dog named Salesman). They were simply never trained to coach.

Do any of these reasons relate to you and your situation? Why? Throughout this book, we hope to make the process of coaching easier for you to understand and implement so that coaching becomes a top priority (if it is not already), and so that it becomes a great way for you to build greatness in yourself or in your team members.

Now we know that coaching matters; we know the difference between a boss and coach; we understand the benefits of coaching and why it does not always happen. Next we will ask you to look in the mirror and see how you or your coach measures up when compared to top sales coaches.

Assessment vs. Top Performers

After working with 500,000 salespeople and 10,000 of their coaches, we have come up with a representative list of top sales coach best practices. Read through the following assessment and rate your or your coach's performance in each of the behaviors that top sales coaches demonstrate consistently. If you are a sales coach, rank yourself; if you are a salesperson, rank the person that leads your team. Mark each area:

3 = Excellent   2 = Meets Expectations   1 = Poor

____ Enthusiasm. You (or your coach) have a positive attitude, are optimistic, and believe in your people and yourself. The room gets brighter when you enter it, not when you leave it.

____ People skills. You communicate succinctly, are perceived as friendly, a good listener, and as one who establishes trust and credibility quickly.

____ Organization/planning. You plan your work and work your plan; you operate in an organized manner and have systems and processes in place to do your job. Others know what to expect from you, and this gives them the ability to execute.

____ Goal setting meetings. You conduct consistent and meaningful one-on-one goal-setting meetings with members of your sales team to monitor the progress of mutually agreed-upon action plans. You and your salespeople can track their professional development as a result of these meetings.

____ Training. You are effective at teaching others to do the job so that they perform at a high level.

____ Follow-up. You check in on a consistent basis and deliver the appropriate type of feedback that holds people accountable and keeps people moving toward their goals in a positive way.

____ Coaching in the crunch. You lead from the trenches by doing the job with your people on real prospects and customers and can comfortably play the role of leader, supporter, or observer on sales calls and/or over the phone.

____ Team meetings. You conduct consistent meetings that people are motivated to attend, that incorporate recognition, and that leave people inspired to hit their goals.

____ Knowledge. You know the products, the market, technical information, prospects and customers, and the industry so that your people can use you as a resource that instills confidence in all team members.

____ Flexibility. You are able to adapt in order to manage top performers and underperformers, different personalities, and work through changes in the market and industry.

Add up your score. If you scored a 30 or higher, you need to either: a) draw an extra line, write "Humility" next to the line, and write a "1" over it; or b) polish your math skills.

If you scored 24–29, wow! We could have used your help writing this book. You will love reading ahead, because doing so will give you the validation that you are already doing a lot of the right things, and you will pick up a few new ideas to implement very easily.

If you scored 17–23, fantastic! You've probably been a sales coach for a while and/or you've had some effective coaches yourself. This book will help you refine skills and habits so that you perform at the highest levels.

If you scored 10–16, there's only one direction to go from here. Begin implementing the best practices from this book one at a time and watch your confidence and results soar!

In summary, we have examined the strong impact a coach can have and defined the role of a coach versus that of a traditional boss or manager. Next, we presented the coaching model that the best sales organizations implement to create great salespeople over and over again. We also outlined the benefits of coaching and listed reasons why coaching is sometimes avoided. And finally, you ranked yourself or your coach on the skills and abilities used by the best sales coaches. Now it's time to become great ourselves. Let's get started!

"You don't have to be great to start; you have to start to be great."
—Unknown, but we like it, so we may
take credit from this day forward

2 | Planning— The Foundation of Coaching

The Coaching Model

In our effort to create a great salesperson, we will consistently refer to the same coaching model shown in Chapter 1. As you can see from Figure 2.1, the starting point in the coaching model is planning, so that's where we'll begin. Since selling is everyone's business, and the best salespeople plan, planning is everyone's business too.

Summary of the World

If we could shrink the Earth's population to a village of precisely 100 people, with the existing ratio of nationalities remaining the

FIGURE 2.1   Coaching Model 02

same, it would look like this: There would be 57 Asians, 21 Europeans, 14 individuals from the Western Hemisphere, including North and South America, and 8 individuals from Africa. Fifty-one would be female and 49 would be male. Seventy would be non-white, while 30 would be white. Sixty-six would be non-Christian and 33 Christian. Eighty would live in substandard housing. Seventy would be unable to read. Half would suffer from malnutrition. One would be near death, and one would be near birth. Only one would have a college education. Half of the entire village's wealth would be in the hands of only six people, and all six would be citizens of the United States.

So if you can read (and we hope you can because this book does not have many pictures), you have a leg up on 70 percent of the world's population. And if you are fortunate enough to have a college degree, you have an advantage that 99 percent of the world does not have. If you live in the United States (about 2 percent of the world's population), you have direct access to half the world's wealth and financial opportunity. If you have any of these things going for you (or all of them for many of you), we'd argue that you can be successful by accident! In fact, some of you may be nodding your head right now because you know someone who has become successful by accident. Imagine if you put together a great plan for yourself or your team and you set yourself up to succeed *on purpose*. With these odds in your favor, and a great plan to succeed on purpose, any accomplishment should be a no-brainer.

According to Eleanor Roosevelt, "It takes as much energy to wish as it does to plan." We all wish, so let's look at some of the benefits of planning.

There are many specific benefits for the salesperson or sales coach who has a written business plan. Some of the more significant ones are also the most beneficial:

- You work more efficiently and have strong time management skills because you know what to do when you arrive at work each day. Specific activities are outlined in your overall plan. You get to execution more quickly because you have streamlined the preliminary stages of planning.
- You have less stress, and you are less likely to stay up at night thinking about the next day or week, so you enjoy your time more when you are not working. An advisor once told us that we all have a superhighway of information in our heads. The cars are all the ideas. To control the traffic, when you think about an important idea, write it down in your plan and park the cars.
- You stay focused on what's most important because you have deliberately taken the time to think through the processes of your day and identify the priorities.
- You create a benchmarking tool against which you can measure your daily, weekly, and monthly results. You always know where you stand.
- You force yourself to have the discipline to take time to think and plan.
- You are prepared for challenges before they arise, so you have fewer fires to address. You are a fire preventer, not a fire fighter.

There are many other benefits from planning. In fact, there are already entire books written on planning, so we are not going to continue to enumerate the benefits here.

WIN

(AHS) My first great sales coach in a professional setting was a woman named Jamie McIntosh. Jamie was my coach when I was a salesperson, and as we both were promoted she continued to coach me when I became a sales coach. Like most new sales coaches, when I first took on the role I was excited but quickly became overwhelmed. With so many responsibilities, I was not sure where my focus should be. Should I devote my time to customer service issues, sales and marketing, coaching my people, planning, or recruiting? I had no clue, so I tried to do it all every day. My performance was similar to that of a rocking chair—lots of motion with no progress. Jamie sat down with me, and we constructed a yearly plan that outlined what I wanted my business to look like one year from that point. We set several incremental goals along the way and wrote down specific action steps that we determined I would have to accomplish to hit my goals. At the end of the meeting Jamie handed me one of her business cards and wrote the letters W-I-N on the back. She explained that the acronym meant "What's Important Now?" Every time I was unsure of where to invest my time, I pulled out my business plan, and the decision of what to focus on next became much easier. Years later, I still carry the card in my wallet and refer to it whenever I have to make decisions or prioritize tasks in my professional or personal life. Having a plan as your compass, whether you are a coach or a salesperson, enables you to make decisions day-to-day, and helps you stay honest with yourself by staying committed to activities that support the plan.

Obviously a coach must "walk the walk" and implement a plan for himself as well as help create plans for his sales team members.

There are many benefits a coach receives when he has his salespeople create a written plan:

- The coach understands what motivates each of his people personally and professionally. This knowledge positively impacts retention because it keeps a focus on the big picture and helps build the coach–salesperson relationship.

- An agreement between the coach and salesperson to focus on the plan centers the coaching relationship. This agreement provides the foundation for communication throughout the year and prevents miscommunication or ambiguity. Both parties share ownership of the goals and the plan.

- The coach uses the plan as a compass that helps guide salespeople back on the right track when they stray.

- The plan provides a context for regular dialogues and feedback that will improve performance. Having a plan enables dialogue and feedback to be more specific and constructive. When feedback is specific, it is acted upon more easily.

- The business plan sets clear performance expectations for both the coach and the salesperson.

- When a salesperson writes down her plan, the coach can more easily hold her accountable to the goals that she set for her business.

- If everyone on the team has a plan, the coach can conduct an extremely effective meeting by having each salesperson give a short business plan presentation at the start of the year. This is motivating for everyone and sets up peer accountability.

While there are significant benefits to business planning, there are a few common pitfalls that coaches and salespeople must avoid during the planning process.

- Often plans are created at the beginning of a fiscal year and then not revisited until it's time to create the plan for the next fiscal year. Both coach and salesperson must keep in mind that the business plan is a process, not an event. The plan must be very visible and be the context for regular dialogue between coach and salesperson.
- The goals in the plan can be set too high or too low. A goal that's too high is demotivating for both coach and salesperson. A goal that's too low means that someone is not being given the opportunity to reach full potential. The best solution to this challenge is that the coach and salesperson must mutually agree on goals. The goals should be based on real data, if at all possible, from past years for that salesperson or from other salespeople in similar situations.
- The last common pitfall is that often a plan is not written down formally. Coach and salesperson discuss ideas at the start of a year and take informal notes if at all. This approach makes it impossible to follow up effectively. As many of our clients tell us: "If it's not written down, it doesn't exist."

Reading this book, you may have a plan, or you may not. Either way, a great first or next step is to have a business plan interview with your coach (if you're a salesperson) or with your salespeople (if you're a coach). This interview is a natural segue into the business planning process. Conducting an interview also creates a connection, which is critical. Most sales organizations see employee retention as an area they constantly strive to improve. Exit interview studies show time and time again that one of the primary reasons people leave their jobs is because of their direct supervisor. As Kevin Kelley, Assistant Vice President of Enterprise Fleet Services, a division of Enterprise Rent-A-Car explains: "If I quit, I quit my manager. The baseline always comes back to how well do you know your people? If you understand their individual visions, you can always come back to what's most important." The business plan interview provides a context for this important discussion. Figure 2.2 is an example of a business plan interview template that a coach could use with a salesperson. You can view other examples on our website at www.nextlevelsalesconsulting.com.

The figure shows a representative list of general questions in a business plan interview. Obviously, you can customize questions to your business. Do your best to keep the questions as open-ended as possible, so that the salesperson shares as much as possible. Also, be sure to take notes in order to demonstrate your genuine interest in the salesperson's plan, and also because the information will likely be very helpful in future coaching interactions.

After the business plan interview is conducted, it is appropriate for a coach to provide a template or example of a business plan so that the salesperson can begin to write one. Keep in mind that the business plan does not need to be a 200-page document. Some of the best plans we've seen are on one or two pages.

Keeping in mind that this is not a book on business planning, we will provide some sample sections of a business plan and explain what each section means. For more specific examples, you can visit our company's website at www.nextlevelsalesconsulting.com.

Business Plan Interview

Date _____

Coach_____ Salesperson _____

Why did you select a career with Acme?

_____

_____

_____

What are your goals for the upcoming year?

_____

_____

_____

What are your career goals with Acme?

_____

_____

_____

What are some of your goals outside of work?

_____

_____

_____

What are your strengths and weaknesses as a salesperson?

_____

_____

_____

FIGURE 2.2 Business Plan Interview

How do you want to improve your skills and abilities this year?

_____

_____

_____

What is your strategy for new business development this year?

_____

_____

_____

What is your strategy for developing business with existing clients this year?

_____

_____

_____

Walk me through a typical day, week, and month of sales activity for you?

_____

_____

_____

What are the biggest challenges you face in growing your business?

_____

_____

_____

How do you like to be coached?

_____

_____

_____

FIGURE 2.2   *(Continued)*

What expectations do you have for me as your coach?

_____
_____
_____

Describe for me how you would like to be trained and followed up with?

_____
_____
_____

How do you learn best? By doing? Listening? Reading? Watching? Experiencing?

_____
_____
_____

What is the best way to give you feedback?

_____
_____
_____

FIGURE 2.2 *(Continued)*

Example of Business Plan Components

The Vision Statement

When you write a vision statement, you begin with the end in mind. You start all your efforts with a clear definition and understanding of where you are going. That means knowing where you are now and where you need to be and the steps that you must take to get there. You can write a one-year vision or a vision for what you expect your business or performance to look like after any number of years.

Mission Statement

Your mission statement is your philosophy or creed. It focuses on the type of businessperson you want to be (character) and what you expect to do (contributions and achievements). It can also include the values or principles that will govern your decision making. You could call a mission statement a constitution. Like the United States Constitution, it is meant to last a long time.

Goals

Having established the objective and future state of your business in your vision statement, you must determine the sequence of actions to get you there and the milestone accomplishments that will indicate that you are on target. Many plans include personal goals, since these can be the true motivators that drive salespeople to success. Family, status, lifestyle, security are all strong underpinnings for business success. Here you also write down and commit to professional goals that move your career forward. Be as specific as you can with these goals, using numbers and dates. Keep in mind also that your goals must be incremental steps that will enable you to achieve your ultimate vision.

Activity Commitments

Here the salesperson defines and commits to the sales activity that she expects she must fulfill to hit her goals and achieve her vision.

Again, this is an example of potential sections in a business plan. You can create your own to align with your business. The point is that when the plan is written down and agreed upon between coach and salesperson, you are setting yourselves up for a successful year before the year even begins.

At The Next Level, we run a consulting firm, and we are also a sales organization. At the start of each year, each team member writes his or her business plan and includes the following:

- Key accomplishments from last year.
- Business vision for upcoming year.
- Specific business goals for upcoming year.
- Specific personal goals for upcoming year.
- Developmental areas to be addressed in the upcoming year.
- Suggestions to improve the company in the upcoming year.

(AHS) As a salesperson at The Next Level, I write my plan, and then get together with my coach and review it to make sure we both agree it is a fair and realistic plan. Then, at our start of the year kickoff meeting, each team member uses his or her business plan to make a short presentation to the rest of the team. The presentation reviews the previous year's accomplishments and overviews the plan for the upcoming year. We each present our individual goals and share how our plan and goals support the team's overall goals. This is a motivating meeting that creates a commitment to each other and to each of our respective plans.

Some sales organizations we work with have taken the business plan agreement between coach and salesperson to a more formal level. We have seen written agreements like the one in Figure 2.3 in organizations where there is a very large ratio of salespersons to coaches, and often high turnover. Figure 2.3 is an example of such

Coach-Salesperson Agreement

PLEASE INITIAL EACH ITEM.

SALESPERSON

- I understand that coaching is being offered to provide me with the tools to enable me to hit the sales goals I wrote down in my business plan.   X_____

- I understand that my commitment to success requires a regular sales meeting and regular one-on-one goal setting meetings with my coach.   X_____

- I understand that I must use my business plan as a compass to help my coach and I stay on track.   X_____

- I will be honest with myself and my coach; as I realize that this will be the foundation of my success in my career.   X_____

- I am committed to performance reporting to my coach, who will help me hold myself accountable to my commitments.   X_____

COACH

- I have met with you to agree on a realistic business plan that supports your goals and is aligned with the goals of our team.   X_____

- I will prepare for and conduct goal setting meetings (GSMs) with you on a consistent schedule.   X_____

- I will provide you with the support you need to take your business to the next level and coach you to enable you to realize your business plan.   X_____

- I will prepare for and hold regular sales meetings.   X_____

PLEASE SIGN BELOW:

_____ Date:_____
Salesperson

_____ Date:_____
Coach

FIGURE 2.3   Coach-Salesperson Agreement

a written agreement. Check out our website for more examples: www.nextlevelsalesconsulting.com.

The right types of salespeople and coaches who are in their jobs for the long haul to be successful are very motivated by this type of a commitment. (AHS) I have had some coaches who had me sign agreements like this and others who did not. As a salesperson, when I sign it I feel a cautious excitement because I want to blow out my goals, and I know I will be held accountable. Like most others, I do not want to let my coach down, and more importantly, I do not want to let myself down. When I've written down a plan and made certain commitments and then hit them; I walk into that next meeting with my coach "feeling money": "Boo-ya coach, how you like me now?" A great coach then channels that enthusiasm toward a higher set of goals and commitments for the next period.

In creating a great salesperson we begin with planning: an interview to create a connection, a written plan that will serve as the foundation for the upcoming year, and a signed agreement to indicate commitment and accountability in both directions. The plan is great, but we still have not really done anything yet.

As Steve Fox, Vice President of Remarketing at Enterprise Rent-A-Car puts it: "Planning is important, but if you can't execute, the plan is worthless. Execution is more important than anything. There's nothing better than planning, executing, and winning. That's fun."

Now it's time to start executing the plan.

3 | Goal-Setting Meetings

If you are a sales coach working to build a great team, or a salesperson working to build a great performer in yourself, and you are going to read only one chapter from this book, we suggest that this be the one. To summarize the first two chapters, we understand that coaching is important and can have a significant positive impact on a salesperson's or a sales team's performance. We have a plan in place that both coach and salesperson agree can lead toward success. In all the coach-salesperson relationships we have observed, we have found that the most effective means the best coaches use to keep their people focused on their plans is to have regular goal-setting meetings. A goal-setting meeting (GSM) is a consistent, scheduled one-on-one meeting between salesperson and coach, in which the duo reviews performance from the previous period and creates and commits to a game plan and short-term action steps for the upcoming period. (We will use "period" as the regular time length between GSMs because the length of

31

the period can vary from situation to situation depending on several factors, which we will discuss later. Most top coaches conduct GSMs weekly or monthly with each team member.) Refer to the coaching model shown in Figure 3.1 to see that the first GSM happens soon after the initial creation of and agreement on the business plan.

FIGURE 3.1   Coaching Model 3

The Coaching Model

If all salespeople just wrote down a plan at the beginning of the year and executed it flawlessly, the coach's job would be about as easy as a gravy train on biscuit wheels rolling down the hill in the shade. Sorry, most don't do that. Most people face challenges in executing all aspects of their plan. You probably know some of these underperformers:

- Confused Cathy. She doesn't understand the organization's priorities. Cathy may have talent and skills and a strong work ethic but she is channeling her energy in the wrong directions. We work with several financial services firms, many of which have corporate initiatives to open new accounts greater than $100,000. Cathy is bringing in several new accounts each week, but the majority of them are under $100,000.
- Unskilled Ursula. She's got the will, commitment, and focus, but not the skills to get the job done. Often new salespeople fall into this category. While Ursula may be the first in each morning and the last to leave and be excited to make telephone calls all day, she is not able to hit her goals because she does not have the skills to get past the gatekeeper.
- Complacent Chris. He has all the skills and abilities but he lacks the will and commitment to achieve his potential. Chris is content with mediocrity. He converts prospects to customers at a high rate. He just does not talk to enough prospects.
- Lost Larry. He does not have all the tools and resources to do the job most effectively. Larry may have access to the tools,

but is unwilling to learn how to use them. He is not willing
to invest the time to learn the new online lead management
system that all other salespeople are having success with.

- Victim Vince. He is cynical and blames everyone but the guy
  in the mirror for his lack of performance. "I would hit all my
  goals if it were not for my co-workers, internal business partners, poor leads, bad territory, bad accounts, terrible products, and our weak technology."

If you are a sales coach, or aspire to be one, you owe Cathy,
Ursula, Chris, Larry, and Vince a thank you, because without them
you would be jobless. Fortunately, you have GSMs as a tool in
your arsenal to keep people, like the ones above, more focused on
their plans.

The Purpose of Goal-Setting Meetings

*"The real purpose of these meetings is to establish goals for the
month and determine what the salesperson is going to do to hit
them and what the manager is going to do to support that effort."*
                        —Tom Chelew, Vice President of
                             Fleet Services at Enterprise
                             Rent-A-Car

Goal-setting meetings are important for many reasons:

- GSMs open up communication between coaches and salespeople. Since the meeting is a regular structured time that
  forces communication, a relationship develops.

- They enable coaches to be more proactive. When there are regular meetings already on the calendar for coach and salesperson, the salesperson knows that he will have that time with his coach. As a result, he does not come running into the coach's office sporadically all week or month, he waits until his meeting. The coach has fewer fires to put out and can anticipate future problems or needs.
- They provide opportunities to set and periodically reexamine agreed-upon priorities. The best coaches and salespeople often refer to their yearly business plans during these regular GSMs to make sure week-to-week and month-to-month actions are in line with the bigger picture.
- They provide opportunities for training. Throughout the month or during a GSM, a coach will identify certain skill issues. Some coaches will actually conduct short one-on-one training sessions within the GSM, while others use the GSM to schedule separate individual or team training sessions to address skill issues.
- They give salespeople the opportunity to voice any concerns in a private setting. Some important issues will never be brought to the coach's attention if the salesperson is never given one-on-one time with the coach.
- They give the coach the opportunity to motivate and inspire a salesperson. Great coaches use these meetings to provide long-term perspective for salespeople to keep them thinking big.

Goal-Setting Meeting Guidelines

A wealthy landowner made a fascinating discovery when he was checking employee records and called a longtime employee into his study. "Peter," asked the billionaire real estate tycoon, "how long have you been with us now?" "Almost 25 years," replied the employee. His employer frowned. "According to these records, you were hired to take care of the stables." "That's correct sir," said Peter. "But we haven't owned horses for more than 20 years," said his boss. "Right, sir. What would you like me to do next?"

—*The Executive Speechwriter Newsletter,*
Volume 13, Number 3

For goal-setting meetings to be effective, you should probably conduct the one-on-one meetings more frequently than every 20 years, since most top coaches believe that the best way to spend their time is in developing their people. To ensure that GSMs are maintained as a top priority, here are some general guidelines:

- GSMs are typically 30 to 60 minutes long, depending on several factors including frequency, experience of salesperson, performance, and personality.
- Top sales coaches tend to hold GSMs with each salesperson at least once a month. Geography, salesperson tenure, performance, and ratio of coaches to salespeople can all impact the frequency of GSMs.
- GSMs are typically planned and scheduled in advance. The best sales coaches and salespeople treat scheduled GSMs the same way they would a meeting with a hot prospect. It is planned in advance, confirmed, and rescheduled only due to an emergency.
- Meetings should be documented on a standardized form. This is critical for several reasons. Primarily, a trail of documented GSM forms will enable a coach or salesperson to

look back over several weeks and months and track progress. This data is excellent to use in more formal reviews and for promotion decisions. If performance goes in the wrong direction consistently, the coach may also be glad to have documentation for Human Resources to support a termination decision. Lastly, documentation from GSMs serves as a tool for follow-up for both parties. It enables the salesperson to hold himself personally accountable, because he will have his goals from the meeting displayed in his work area. The coach now has specific areas to follow up on until the next GSM and, most importantly, at the next GSM. We'll dig much deeper into this follow-up in Chapter 5.

- Keep GSMs uninterrupted. An uninterrupted meeting shows the coach's commitment to the salesperson's development and makes it clear that the GSM is a priority. Many coaches conduct GSMs out of the office or in a conference room to avoid distractions.

The Goal-Setting Meeting Agenda

Most effective coaches follow a flow or agenda in their GSMs like the one suggested here. Having a consistent approach to these meetings tends to work well for the coach and the salesperson because both know what to expect, no time is wasted figuring out what to do, and both come prepared. Here is the structure that has been proven to work for many of the sales coaches we have observed:

- Presentation of the Agenda.
- Discovery.

- Solution and Game Plan.
- Summary and Commitment.
- Encouragement.

We've discussed the importance of documenting these meetings. See Figure 3.2, which is a sample of a documentation tool. As we move through the GSM process in this chapter, we will define and give examples of each step, and also explain how to effectively document each portion of the meeting.

> *"Give me a stock clerk with a goal and I will give you a man who will make history. Give me a man without a goal, and I will give you a stock clerk!"*
>
> —J.C. Penney

GSMs focus on goals within certain key performance indicators, or KPIs. KPIs are those areas that will move team members toward the team vision, and move salespeople toward achieving their individual goals and realizing their business plans. Therefore, it is critical that the coach has regular communication with each team member about his performance in each KPI. Here are a few sample KPIs from some of the industries where we have spent time recently:

- KPIs for a financial advisor at a financial services firm: contacts, appointments held, secured assets, referrals gained, and revenue.
- KPIs for an account executive in the mortgage industry: loan applications, loans funded, funding ratio, sales volume, and number of sales calls.

GOAL-SETTING MEETING

SALESPERSON: _____   COACH: _____   DATE: _____

REVIEW OF LAST MEETING ACTION STEPS:

_____
_____
_____
_____

Key Metric	Goal	Actual	+/−	New Goal

OBSERVATIONS:

_____
_____
_____

ACTION STEPS:

1. _____
2. _____
3. _____

EXPECTED HELP FROM COACH/ACTION STEPS:

_____
_____
_____

SALESPERSON SIGNATURE: **COACH SIGNATURE:**

_____   _____

Next Meeting Date: Time:

_____   _____

FIGURE 3.2   Goal-Setting Meeting

- KPIs for a salesperson in the travel industry: marketing hours, sales calls, service calls, and marketing lunches.
- KPIs for a sales consultant at The Next Level on his GSM form: appointments held, site visits conducted, proposals delivered, signed proposals, and billable days.

"You have to expect things of yourself before you can do them."
—Michael Jordan

The goal within each KPI becomes the expectation to be fulfilled between goal setting meetings. If a salesperson hits the periodic goals that are set in the GSMs, she should achieve her business plan.

Before we break down each step of the GSM, we will present an overview of the process in Figure 3.3. This overview can serve as the coach's job aid while conducting GSMs.

GSM Step 1: Presentation of the Agenda

Successful coaches begin goal-setting meetings by building rapport with the salesperson through preliminary pleasantries. Before discussing KPIs and goals, great coaches take a moment to build the relationship by asking about family, hobbies, or the progress of a local sports team like the Maryland Terrapins. The coach may also share something about his life outside of work.

After building rapport, the coach begins the GSM on a positive note by using an agenda statement to establish a clear focus. This helps the coach be more direct and improves his ability to

The Basic GSM Meeting Process

STEP 1 – PRESENTATION OF THE AGENDA

BEGIN DIALOGUE WITH AN AGENDA STATEMENT

- Purpose of meeting
- Review of last GSM goals and action steps
- Review key performance indicators (KPIs)
- Build a game plan
- Gain input on agenda from your salesperson

STEP 2 – DISCOVERY

ASK QUESTIONS CONCERNING

- Action steps from last GSM
- Expectations/goals vs. actual performance
- What's working/not working
- Document observations
- Discovery summary

STEP 3 – SOLUTION AND GAME PLAN

BUILD A GAME PLAN UNTIL THE NEXT GSM

- Set clear action steps for the salesperson
- Set clear action steps for the coach
- The solution/game plan ideally comes from the salesperson with accountability or the coach can recommend a solution/game plan that the salesperson agrees to execute
- Document SMART action steps

STEP 4 – SUMMARY AND COMMITMENT

REVIEW THE ACTION PLAN

- Salesperson reviews goals
- Salesperson reviews action steps
- Coach reviews her action steps
- Set date and time of next GSM

STEP 5 – ENCOURAGEMENT

AFFIRM CONFIDENCE IN YOUR SALESPERSON

- Express your optimism
- Be sincere and specific

FIGURE 3.3   The Basic GSM Meeting Process

keep the meeting on track. This technique will ensure that coach and salesperson are focused on addressing the same issue(s). Remember, if the salesperson is not performing well, he will want to talk about everything else under the sun except performance. If the coach uses a clear agenda, that problem should be eliminated. Setting the agenda to start a GSM is very similar to the way successful salespeople set the agenda to start a sales call.

Set the Agenda Example

Coach: Melissa, I'm glad we have a few minutes to work together this morning. Did you see that Tech game this weekend?

Salesperson: Yeah. Let's go Hokies.

Coach: So, let's get started. The purpose of our meeting is to come up with a plan to keep you on track with your business plan. In order to maximize our time, I suggest we follow this agenda:

First, let's review how you did on last week's action steps. Then we can look at your performance for last week. After that we can set some goals for next week, and we can come up with some action steps and a game plan to get you there.

Is there anything you would like to add to that?

Salesperson: No.

Coach: Great. Then why don't we start by reviewing how you did on last week's action steps?

After this exchange, the coach moves to discovery questions.

GSM Step 2: Discovery

According to dictionaries, discovery is *to gain sight or knowledge of*. As a coach asks questions about last period's GSM commitments, he should be able to quickly gain knowledge and insight into how successful or unsuccessful the salesperson has been. Stephen Covey agrees with this approach of asking questions first: "Seek first to understand, then to be understood." (See Figure 3.4.)

The coach begins the GSM by reviewing the action steps established in the last GSM; this is a great opportunity to deliver positive recognition if the salesperson has completed his action steps. If he has not, the coach can dig a bit deeper with questions to determine if a skill or will issue may exist. This could be an opportunity to provide some constructive feedback. If an action step was not completed, it can carry over and become an action step for the upcoming period. Remember, this accountability is huge for the salesperson and for the coach because all the action steps set at the last GSM support the salesperson's goals, which support his business plan.

By looking at two examples of action steps, you will learn some key criteria to keep in mind when setting them.

Example One: Review of Last Meeting Action Steps

Generate more referral business.

Conduct more sales calls each week.

GOAL-SETTING MEETING

SALESPERSON: _____   COACH: _____   DATE: _____

REVIEW OF LAST MEETING ACTION STEPS:

_____
_____
_____
_____

Key Metric	Goal	Actual	+/–	New Goal

OBSERVATIONS:

_____
_____
_____

ACTION STEPS:

1. _____
2. _____
3. _____

EXPECTED HELP FROM COACH/ACTION STEPS:

_____
_____
_____

SALESPERSON SIGNATURE: **COACH SIGNATURE:**

_____   _____

Next Meeting Date: Time:

_____   _____

FIGURE 3.4   Goal-Setting Meeting

In this example, the coach can begin discovery by asking the salesperson how things went last month with referrals and sales calls. The coach will probably get an answer like, "I tried to get some more referrals, and that seems to be going well. And I've definitely been getting out on more sales calls lately. I've been busy."

Example Two: Review of Last Meeting Action Steps

Create Fogel proposal after 2 P.M. Friday.

Make at least 50 marketing calls Mon. and Wed. 8–10 A.M.

In example two, the coach can begin discovery by asking about the status of the Fogel proposal and about the marketing calls. Now the coach may get an answer like, "I wrote the Fogel proposal and I feel really confident now. The meeting to present it is tomorrow. I made a total of 106 marketing calls combined on Monday and Wednesday, so I feel good about that too."

What is the difference between the action steps in the two examples? In example two they are specific enough that it is easy for the salesperson to know that he has completed the actions, and it is easy for the coach to follow up and hold him accountable. We will discuss the importance of setting specific goals a bit later.

At this point in the meeting, salespeople should be feeling great if they completed their action steps, pretty good if they put forth a strong effort and just fell short, and a bit uncomfortable if they did not put forth the effort. Remember, if you are a salesperson and you feel uncomfortable because you didn't do what you had committed to, that's a good thing. You want to be successful and follow through in the future. If you are a coach and you are asking questions to create some discomfort in the salesperson who did not complete his action steps, you are doing so because you want him and your team to become successful and achieve your business plans. Keep in mind that the purpose of the GSM is to build people up and keep them motivated, but a little discomfort is acceptable.

Once you have asked enough questions to understand the status of the last GSM's action steps, you continue asking discovery questions to learn about the key performance indicators. (See Figure 3.5.)

(SRJ) I have a long-time friend and running partner named Phil. Phil and I used to go out a lot on the weekends before I got married and started a family. Now we do not go out as much, but we still run together. One particular Sunday morning Phil and I were headed out on a run, and I decided to bring my three-year old son Matthew along in the baby jogger. A couple of miles into our run, Matthew looked up at me from the jogger and asked: "Where's Phil?" "Phil's a little behind us, Matthew." "Why is he behind us?" "Because daddy has longer legs than Phil." "Why?" "Because daddy's taller than Phil." A few minutes passed before Matthew perked up again: "Where's Phil?" "He's still behind us." "Why?" "Because daddy has longer legs." "Why?" "Because I'm taller." Later, Matthew asks again: "Where's Phil?" "He's still behind us." "Why?" "All right, Matthew. Phil's behind us because he went to Pancho's last night and had seven Cadillac margaritas and six shots of José Cuervo Gold. Daddy went to bed at nine o'clock last night and got up early and ate a box of Wheaties!"

GOAL-SETTING MEETING

SALESPERSON: <u>MELISSA</u>   COACH: <u>KEVIN</u>   DATE: <u>AUGUST 1, 2005</u>

REVIEW OF LAST MEETING ACTION STEPS:

Create Fogel proposal after 2 PM Friday—Done
Make at least 50 marketing calls Mon and Wed 8–10 AM—Done total of 106

Key Metric	Goal	Actual	+/−	New Goal
Cold Calls	100	106	+6	
Appointments Set	5	4	−1	
Presentations	2	2	−	
Closed Accounts	1	1	−	

OBSERVATIONS:

ACTION STEPS:

1.
2.
3.

EXPECTED HELP FROM COACH/ACTION STEPS:

SALESPERSON SIGNATURE: **COACH SIGNATURE:**

Next Meeting Date: Time:

FIGURE 3.5   Goal-Setting Meeting

Most children could teach any salesperson or coach a lesson in asking discovery questions. Just like Matthew, your job in asking questions during a GSM is to uncover the root of why the salesperson is hitting her goals or why she is not. As the coach, you try to ask more questions and speak less. The coach should be like a field of corn—all ears. Go down the form, one KPI at a time, and engage in dialogue to learn what happened. In the previous example, Kevin (coach) would be taking notes as he interviewed Melissa (salesperson) about her recent performance. Here's a representative list of questions you the coach can may ask:

- What were your results?
- What worked well for you?
- What enabled you to be successful and exceed the goal?
- What obstacles did you encounter?
- How did you overcome them?
- What did you learn?
- Why was there a shortfall?
- What are your goals between now and our next GSM?

When there are shortfalls in a salesperson's performance, and if the coach is asking all the right questions, the challenge will typically boil down to either a skill issue or a will issue. (See coaching model at start of chapter.) With a skill issue, the salesperson is motivated and has the required work ethic to succeed, but he has not yet learned all the skills or developed the abilities required to hit his goals. The coach will address skill issues with training in a variety of different contexts, coaching in the crunch (when coach and salesperson do the job together), and follow-up and feedback. These topics will be discussed in detail in the next chapters. With a will issue, the salesperson may have the skills and abilities required to hit his goals but is just not motivated or putting forth the effort to achieve success. The coach will address will issues with a combination of goal setting, accelerated (more regular) GSMs, and follow-up with feedback.

If you are a sports fan and like to follow a particular team, you may check the box scores in the newspaper to see how your team performed. The box score, as you can see in the example in Figure 3.6, shows all the numbers and statistics from a particular game. (Our friend and colleague Bob Coakley, from Lowell, Massachusetts asked us to include this particular box score and

Boston 17, NY Yankees 1 — Today's Boxes 5/28/05

May 28, 2005

	1	2	3	4	5	6	7	8	9	R	H	E
Boston	1	2	0	2	7	0	2	3	0	17	27	1
NY Yankees	0	0	0	0	0	0	1	0	0	1	8	0

Boston (26-22) Won 1 — NY Yankees (27-22) Lost 1

Boston	AB	R	H	RBI	BB	SO	LOB	AVG
Damon, CF	7	3	4	1	0	0	2	.345
Renteria, SS	3	2	3	5	0	0	0	.281
a-Vazquez, PH-SS	3	1	1	0	0	1	2	.239
Ortiz, DH	4	3	2	1	2	1	3	.281
Ramirez, M, LF	4	1	4	1	0	0	0	.243
Payton, LF	2	2	1	3	0	0	2	.228
Nixon, RF	6	1	3	5	0	0	0	.316
Varitek, C	5	1	2	0	0	1	2	.329
Shoppach, C	0	0	0	0	0	0	0	.000
Olerud, 1B	6	0	3	1	0	0	2	.500
Mueller, 3B	4	1	2	0	0	1	4	.289
1-Youkilis, PR -3B	2	0	0	0	0	0	4	.324
Bellhorn, 2B	6	2	2	0	0	1	3	.241
Totals	**52**	**17**	**27**	**17**	**2**	**5**	**26**	

NY Yankees	AB	R	H	RBI	BB	SO	LOB	AVG
Jeter, SS	1	0	0	0	0	1	0	.304
a-Sanchez, PH-SS	3	0	0	0	0	0	1	.323
Womack, LF	5	1	2	0	0	1	1	.275
Sheffield, RF	1	0	0	0	1	1	0	.316
b-Sierra, R, PH-RF	3	0	0	0	0	0	2	.219
Matsui, CF	2	0	0	0	1	0	2	.264
c-Williams, PH-CF	3	0	2	1	0	0	0	.239
Rodriguez, A, 3B	2	0	2	0	1	0	0	.331
Johnson, 3B	1	0	1	0	0	0	0	.250
Martinez, 1B	3	0	0	0	1	0	6	.258
Giambi, DH	3	0	1	0	1	1	4	.222
Flaherty, C	4	0	0	0	0	2	5	.222
Cano, 2B	4	0	0	0	0	1	3	.250
Totals	**35**	**1**	**8**	**1**	**4**	**8**	**24**	

Boston	IP	H	R	ER	BB	SO	HR	ERA
Clement (W,6-0)	6.0	5	0	0	4	7	0	3.0
Timlin	1.0	3	1	1	0	1	0	1.5
Myers	1.0	0	0	0	0	0	0	2.3
Foulke	1.0	0	0	0	0	0	0	6.6

NY Yankees	IP	H	R	ER	BB	SO	HR	ERA
Pavano (L, 4-3)	3.2	11	5	5	1	2	0	4.18
Stanton	0.2	3	3	3	0	1	0	7.36
Quantrill	2.2	7	6	6	1	2	3	6.53
Groom	2.0	6	3	3	0	0	0	6.59

NEW YORK – The Yankees entered Saturday's game with 16 wins in their last 18 games, thanks largely to their starting pitchers, who went 15-1 with 2.93 ERA in that span.

Saturday, Carl Pavano didn't live up to the rotation's reputation, getting hit hard during his 3 2/3-inning outing as the Red Sox hammered the Yankees, 17-1 at Yankee Stadium. The right-hander was charged with five runs on 11 hits, falling to 4-3.

Boston pounded New York pitching for 27 hits in the game, scoring seven runs in the fifth inning against Mike Stanton and Paul Quantrill to break the game wide oped three homers, includinan Edgar Renteria grand slam and a three-run shot by Trot Nixon in the fifth inning.

Pavano allowed a run in the first and two more in the second, putting New York in a quick 3-0 hole. The Sox added two more in the forth on two-out RBI singles by Manny Ramirez and Nixon, knockingfrom the game after just 3 2/3 innings. It was Pavano's shortest non-injury outing since June 27, 2003, when he gave up six runs without getting an out – against the Red Sox.

The seven-run gave the Sox a 12-0 lead, prompting the Yankees to remove several of their starting players for a few innings of rest.

Matt Clement (6-0) ad little trouble making the runs stand up, limiting the Yankees to two hits over the first four innings. The Yankees loaded the bases in the fifth, but Clement got Tino Martinez toending the team's only real threat of the afternoon.

Quantrill allowed his third homer in the seventh as Jay Payton blasted a two-run shot. Boston tacked on three more in the eighth to cap the scoring. Bernie Williams singles in Tony Womack in thesnap the shutout bid.

FIGURE 3.6 Red Sox v. Yankees Box Score

game summary.) This section is analogous to the KPI numbers that a coach reviews with a salesperson in a GSM. Below the box score is a short game summary with more detail on exactly what happened during the game to produce the numbers above. This section is analogous to the observations portion of the GSM form. As the coach asks questions regarding the previous GSM's action steps and the KPIs, he takes notes very carefully to capture the entire story (see example in Figure 3.7). This information is critical in developing focused goals and action steps for the next period.

Once the coach has asked enough questions to gain a crystal clear understanding of the status of last GSM's action steps and KPIs, it is almost time to create goals and action steps for the next period. Before creating the game plan, though, it is important that the coach make a brief summary to confirm that all the documentation is accurate. (See Figure 3.7.) Here is an example of what that brief summary could sound like:

> *Coach:* Let's review your last week to make sure I understand everything. You're all set with your Fogel proposal and are presenting tomorrow. You exceeded your call goal by six and have more opportunity to call from that abc.com directory. You missed your appointment goal by one, nailed your presentation goal, and most importantly, closed that Schultz deal for forty thousand. All in all, a very solid week! Is that everything?
>
> *Salesperson:* Yes. That was my week.
>
> *Coach:* Great. Let's put together a plan so that this upcoming week is strong also.

GOAL-SETTING MEETING

SALESPERSON: <u>MELISSA</u>   COACH: <u>KEVIN</u>   DATE: <u>AUGUST 1, 2005</u>

REVIEW OF LAST MEETING ACTION STEPS:

Create Fogel proposal after 2 PM Friday—Done
Make at least 50 marketing calls Mon and Wed 8–10 AM—Done total of 106

Key Metric	Goal	Actual	+/−	New Goal
Cold Calls	100	106	+6	
Appointments Set	5	4	−1	
Presentations	2	2	−	
Closed Accounts	1	1	−	

OBSERVATIONS:

Feeling good about Fogel presentation on 8/2. Built list for marketing calls from abc.com directory. Seems to be a great resource. Closed deal with Schultz account for $40,000. Has one appointment set for every day this week, except Thursday.

ACTION STEPS:

1.
2.
3.

EXPECTED HELP FROM COACH/ACTION STEPS:

SALESPERSON SIGNATURE: **COACH SIGNATURE:**

Next Meeting Date: Time:

FIGURE 3.7   Goal-Setting Meeting

GSM Step 3: Solution and Game Plan

Our friend Bob has been married to his wife Jennine for two years now. About a year before they were married, when they were thinking about becoming engaged, Bob asked Jennine, "If we decide to get married, how large a ring would you like me to buy you?" Jennine, who has been a very strong salesperson for many years, responded in a nonchalant way: "Bob, it doesn't really matter to me how large a ring you buy me, just so you know that the larger the ring, the easier it will be for other men to see that I'm taken." So now Jennine walks around with a huge rock on her finger because she was very effective at speaking in terms of Bob's interests.

Too often in GSMs, when coaches are working with salespeople to create a game plan for the next period, they set goals and action steps with language such as, "I need you to step that number up to at least 20." Or "Now the goal is 20, can you hit that for me?" Coaches often think and speak in terms of their own interests, not those of the salesperson. These same two sentiments could be communicated with this language: "You get to 20 next month and your quarter will get off to a great start. You'll be even higher than the projections in your business plan." Or "When you hit 20, you'll not only be leading the team, you'll also be much closer to the down payment on that new house." The same information is presented in a much more motivating fashion because it is framed in terms of the salesperson's interests. As coaches work with salespeople to create game plans, they should try to ask questions and present ideas in terms of the salesperson's interests.

Another common challenge coaches face when putting together game plans with their salespeople is taking too much responsibility for the salesperson's plan. . . .

"The responsibility is yours. I will train you, but I won't do the job for you."

—Ward Bassett, sales leader, Maly's
beauty product distributor

(AHS) My brother Jeff, who has become quite a strong salesperson, had an interesting approach to academics at an early age. He was typically an A and B student over the years until one semester when he brought home a couple of Cs on his report card. My parents asked Jeff about the Cs and explained to him that Cs were not acceptable and that they expected him to earn As and Bs. Jeff's response was that it was the teacher's fault he did not earn above a C. He had done his part, so it was clearly the fault of the teacher, who was not teaching effectively enough for him to learn enough to earn an A or B.

This is like a salesperson coming to his coach at the end of the month saying: "I only hit 80 percent of my budget because I was counting on you to help with the other 20 percent." Unacceptable. It is the coach's job to ask the right questions and help make suggestions in the creation of the plan. The coach also may play a part in the salesperson's plan by removing certain obstacles or providing certain resources. It is the salesperson's plan, however, and he or she must own it. As Susie Bechtel, a Division Sales Manager at Maly's, says, "If you're a sales coach, you can't do everything for them (your salespeople). If you're going to do it for them, why do I need them?" Too often coaches take more responsibility for a salesperson's performance than the salesperson does for his own performance. So when creating the plan, the coach needs to walk this fine line of supporting and acting as a resource, without taking ownership over the salesperson's plan. Many coaches have used GSMs to effectively shift the accountability monkey from their backs to the backs of their salespeople. This enables great coaches to teach and lead, not do.

When creating the plan, the coach can ideally guide the salesperson to develop his or her own plan. Coaches do this with focused questions and a belief that salespeople have the ability to solve their own problems, overcome obstacles, and generate improved results. Using questions to draw out the plan from the salesperson is implementing a "pull" strategy. When "pulling," the coach does most of the listening. At the other end of the spectrum is the "push" strategy. "Pushing" is when the coach gives the salesperson ideas and strategies and is very involved in setting goals for her. Using a push strategy, the coach does more of the talking during the construction of a strong game plan. Strong coaches are able to move easily between the two styles and adapt their style to the needs of their salesperson. It is probably most important, as a coach, to be able to read the salesperson and the situation in order to properly determine whether pushing or pulling will be most effective.

The benefits of using pulling techniques to construct a game plan in the right situation with the right salesperson are:

- It is empowering for a salesperson, in a meeting with her coach, to create her own plan. This displays the coach's trust in the salesperson, which is key to a long-term successful coaching relationship.
- There is more accountability. If the salesperson creates her own plan, she will be much more likely to execute it. It's a lot harder to show up at the next GSM and say, "I

didn't do what I said I'd do in the plan I created," than to admit, "I didn't do what you asked me to do in the plan you gave me."

- The salesperson is able to use more of her own creativity in creating the plan, which also enhances ownership.

The benefits of using pushing techniques to construct a game plan in the right situation with the right salesperson are:

- Improved confidence in the plan from the coach and salesperson. The coach is able to refer to his experience over the years or with other salespeople in similar situations. This experience adds credibility and an extra stamp of approval to the coach's plan.
- Time saving. The coach has seen and understood the situation of the salesperson in the past, so he can set the goals and actions steps quickly without having to dig for new and creative ideas.

The drawbacks to using pulling techniques to construct a game plan in the wrong situation with the wrong salesperson are:

- It can be a waste of time to continuously ask questions of a salesperson looking for specific solutions that the salesperson may not be familiar with.
- If a coach tries to pull a plan from a salesperson who does not have enough knowledge or experience to create a plan, the duo could end up with proposed solutions that will not work to achieve the big picture goals and plan.

The drawbacks to using pushing techniques to construct a game plan in the wrong situation with the wrong salesperson are:

- Salespeople can respond to your plan in a negative or defensive manner if they think you are giving them more direction than they need.
- Salespeople will not feel as much ownership over the plan, since it has come from the coach and been given to them.

The Prospector

A prospector was digging for gold without any luck so he decided to go into town and treat himself to a shot of whiskey. He tied his mule to the hitching post and headed into the saloon for a drink. About this time a drunken cowboy staggered out of the bar and said, "Prospector, can you dance?" The prospector said "no." The cowboy fired a bullet into ground by the prospector's feet and the prospector started to dance. Every time he stopped dancing, the cowboy fired another bullet into the ground. After the sixth bullet was fired, the prospector went to his mule, got his shotgun and held it under the cowboy's chin and said, "Cowboy, have you ever kissed a mule?" And the cowboy said, "No, but I've always wanted to."

As the prospector and the cowboy know, you can force people to do things through pushing (and guns), but they will not have a friendly attitude toward you. Over time, to build a great relationship with salespeople, a coach needs to understand when to push and when to pull.

Here are a few examples of bridging statements and questions we have heard successful coaches use in their pushing and pulling.

To push:

- This is what I think you might try.
- Some other successful people on the team have done this.
- People in other branches who are in a similar position, are doing this.

To pull:

- What do you need to do more/less of?
- What do you need to start/stop doing?
- What can you do differently?

(SRJ) For seven years in high school and college I worked for the Mayflower Moving Company on Odessa Avenue in Van Nuys, California. I wore a uniform with green pants and a green shirt with a yellow boat on the back. My friends used to call me Mr. Mayflower. I drove a 35-foot bobtail truck with a lift gate on the back from move to move all through the San Fernando Valley, where the climate is very hot. When I arrived at a home, my associates and I would walk in with the paperwork, a dolly, and moving pads to greet the customer. Then we would search the house and take a mental picture of exactly how we were going to fit all the stuff from the house into the truck. We would always start with the biggest piece of furniture we could find. We would take it out to the truck and put it as far back in the truck as we could. Then we would grab the dolly and a few more moving pads before returning to the house. On top of the large piece of furniture in the back of the truck we would stack chairs and boxes, put pillows and lampshades on top of them, and then seal that portion of the truck off with a mattress. No one ever took a trip in either direction empty-handed, and every item we placed in the truck was done so in a strategic fashion so that it all fit and would remain safe. No energy was wasted and each move we made was aligned with our ultimate goal of a quick and safe move.

A coach and a salesperson can think about their GSM game plans in a similar fashion. Every goal and action step set periodically throughout the year should be aligned with the ultimate goals that are laid out in the business plan. The specific actions steps for both salesperson and coach should also be congruent with the KPI goals. In the first example in Figure 3.8, you will observe goals and actions steps that are very well aligned with the KPI goals at the top of the form. In the example in Figure 3.9, the action steps for the salesperson and coach are completely incongruent with the plan. This does not mean that "studying product knowledge" and "completing the budget" are not important activities that must be done this week. They are just not the action steps that will enable the salesperson to hit her goals. The best coaches place an inordinate amount of emphasis on action steps that are aligned with activity goals because of all the people that fail in sales, 70 percent of them fail due to low activity. People can do the job and be successful; often, they are just not doing the job enough times.

SMART Goals/Action Steps

"A person who aims at nothing is sure to hit it."

—Anonymous

As coach and salesperson work together to construct an action plan, it is critical that the action plan is goal oriented. A goal is a

GOAL-SETTING MEETING

SALESPERSON: __MELISSA__   COACH: __KEVIN__   DATE: __AUGUST 1, 2005__

REVIEW OF LAST MEETING ACTION STEPS:

Create Fogel proposal after 2 PM Friday—Done

Make at least 50 marketing calls Mon and Wed 8–10 AM—Done total of 106

Key Metric	Goal	Actual	+/–	New Goal
Cold Calls	100	106	+6	100
Appointments Set	5	4	–1	6
Presentations	2	2	–	2
Closed Accounts	1	1	–	1

OBSERVATIONS:

Feeling good about Fogel presentation on 8/2. Built list for marketing calls from abc.com directory. Seems to be a great resource. Closed deal with Schultz account for $40,000. Has one appointment set for every day this week, except Thursday.

ACTION STEPS:

1. Continue making calls from abc.com Mon & Wed 8-10—goal of 100 calls.
2. Create Naftaly presentation by Wed 4 PM.
3. Call 10 current clients from "hot list" and ask for referral—goal is 5 names and #s.

EXPECTED HELP FROM COACH/ACTION STEPS:

Dry run on Naftaly presentation with me 4-4:30 Wed.

Call other regions to track down referral scripts by end of day Monday.

SALESPERSON SIGNATURE: COACH SIGNATURE:

Next Meeting Date: Time:

FIGURE 3.8 Goal-Setting Meeting

GOAL-SETTING MEETING

SALESPERSON: MELISSA   **COACH:** KEVIN   **DATE:** AUGUST 1, 2005

REVIEW OF LAST MEETING ACTION STEPS:

Create Fogel proposal after 2 PM Friday—Done

Make at least 50 marketing calls Mon and Wed 8–10 AM—Done total of 106

Key Metric	Goal	Actual	+/−	New Goal
Cold Calls	100	106	+6	100
Appointments Set	5	4	−1	6
Presentations	2	2	−	2
Closed Accounts	1	1	−	1

OBSERVATIONS:

Feeling good about Fogel presentation on 8/2. Built list for marketing calls from

abc.com directory. Seems to be a great resource. Closed deal with Schultz account for

$40,000. Has one appointment set for every day this week, except Thursday.

ACTION STEPS:

1. Study product knowledge for 30 minutes each day after lunch.

2. Complete budget by 4 PM Thursday.

3.

EXPECTED HELP FROM COACH/ACTION STEPS:

Contribute more ideas for phone scripts.

Help to push deals through the internal pipeline.

SALESPERSON SIGNATURE: **COACH SIGNATURE:**

_____   _____

Next Meeting Date: Time:

_____   _____

FIGURE 3.9   Goal-Setting Meeting

specific and measurable accomplishment to be achieved within a specified time. A written goal provides a strong statement of your intent and the results to be achieved. The goal also must include the actions you are going to take that will generate the results you want. Ideally, coaches and salespeople bring their appointment calendar to the GSM so they can put commitments into it during the meeting.

The elements of SMART action steps are shown in Figure 3.10.

(AS) Early in my career as a sales coach, my coach told me that my job was not to be a manager but to be a simplifier. When I met with my salespeople, it was my job to take all the noise and distractions in their professional lives and funnel that into one or two areas of focus. The action steps that are set in each GSM should fulfill the following requirement: If nothing else happens between now

Specific accomplishment to be achieved

Measurable outcome

Action oriented

Realistic

Time specific

FIGURE 3.10   SMART

and the next time we get together for our next GSM, make sure at least these things (action steps) happen. These action steps will be congruent with the KPIs and address any of the skill or will issues that the coach and salesperson identified during the discovery portion of the GSM.

The best coaches are very effective when it comes to setting action steps that are "controllable." If the action step is totally under the control of the salesperson, it is pretty hard to make excuses, and this helps with accountability. For example, one set of action steps might read:

Example #1: Action Steps

1. Close Williams and Goldberg accounts before next Monday's GSM.

    _____

2. Set at least two appointments from foot canvassing.

    _____

The same action steps may also be written like this:

Example #2: Action Steps

1. Role-play Williams and Goldberg presentations, each on a separate member of the sales team, to gain practice. Goal is to close both by next GSM.

    _____

2. Spend three hours foot canvassing Wednesday morning. Goal is at least two appointments.

The salesperson has complete control over whether or not he finds a member of the sales team and schedules time to practice the presentations with him. Investing this time in practice is sure to help the chances of his closing the two accounts. But the salesperson does not have total control over whether or not Williams and Goldberg say yes. Thus action step #1 in example #2 is more effective. With the second action step, the salesperson has much more control over where he spends his time Wednesday morning than he does over whether he sets his two appointments, so again example #2 is more effective. If at the next GSM the salesperson spent the three hours Wednesday morning foot canvassing and only returned with zero or one appointment, the coach can still positively recognize the effort. The coach's next step would probably be to ask more questions to understand what skill issue(s) prevented the salesperson from hitting the appointment goal.

> *"I don't give up on someone until they have given up on themselves. More likely than not, I hired them and found something special then. If someone is regularly committing to action steps and not doing what they said they'd do, I feel badly for them because that means they do not enjoy their job."*
> —Steve Bloom, Senior Vice President
> of Enterprise Fleet Services,
> a division of Enterprise Rent-A-Car

Bloom's comment is especially accurate when the action steps that were set are under the control of the salesperson.

Remember, when setting action steps during a GSM, both parties are very involved. Ideally, there is pushing and pulling happening and not punching or pouncing. At some point in the GSM, the best coaches make sure to ask their salesperson when he wants help from the coach during the period until the next GSM. The action steps that the duo set for the coach should also be controllable, meet the SMART criteria, and be congruent with the KPIs at the top of the documentation tool.

GSM Step 4: Summary and Commitment

After coach and salesperson complete the development of the game plan and action steps for the period, they will move to step 4—summary and commitment. This is a critical step because it is easy to forget all these great ideas as soon as the next phone call comes in. The primary purpose here is to confirm all the action steps and make sure that it is clear who will do what, by what deadline, so that the next GSM is a productive and positive meeting. Some coaches have their salespeople review the plan aloud to make sure both parties are in agreement.

Once the plan is confirmed and reviewed, both salesperson and coach sign the bottom of the form. This signature indicates a commitment and adds one extra layer of accountability. The coach must be a bit careful with the positioning of the signature so that this process is not misinterpreted to be a Human Resources procedure for the company. It's not that at all! This is a documentation tool that both coach and salesperson sign, commit to, and own, so that everyone becomes more successful and realizes their business plans.

The other very simple but important detail at the end of a GSM is to set the next GSM date and time. This helps make the meeting habitual for both salesperson and coach. The GSM process is like the sales process in that it is important to always set the next step. (SRJ) When Elisa, who is now my wife, and I were dating, I would never leave a date without making sure I had the next date.

Here's an example of how this portion of the meeting may sound:

Coach: Great, Melissa. Why don't you review with me your goals and action steps between now and our next GSM?

Salesperson: Sure thing, Kevin. My goals are 100 calls, set six appointments, two presentations, and one new closed account. I'm going to make my calls from 8 to 10 A.M. Monday and Wednesday. I'm also going to complete the Naftaly presentation by Wednesday at four, and make ten referral calls.

Coach: Excellent. I'll be ready to do the Naftaly dry run with you Wednesday at four, and I will get you those referral scripts. I'm committed to another great week. Do I have your commitment to your action steps?

Salesperson: Definitely.

Coach: Let's each sign off. And we'll do our next meeting Monday at 7:30 again, right?

Salesperson: Sounds good. See you then.

Figure 3.11 highlights the section of the GSM documentation tool that the coach and salesperson sign and use to set their next GSM.

GOAL-SETTING MEETING

SALESPERSON: __MELISSA__   COACH: __KEVIN__   DATE: __AUGUST 1, 2005__

REVIEW OF LAST MEETING ACTION STEPS:

Create Fogel proposal after 2 PM Friday—Done
Make at least 50 marketing calls Mon and Wed 8–10 AM—Done total of 106

Key Metric	Goal	Actual	+/−	New Goal
Cold Calls	100	106	+6	100
Appointments Set	5	4	−1	6
Presentations	2	2	−	2
Closed Accounts	1	1	−	1

OBSERVATIONS:

Feeling good about Fogel presentation on 8/2. Built list for marketing calls from abc.com directory. Seems to be a great resource. Closed deal with Schultz account for $40,000. Has one appointment set for every day this week, except Thursday.

ACTION STEPS:

1. Continue making calls from abc.com Mon & Wed 8–10—goal of 100 calls.
2. Create Naftaly presentation by Wed 4 PM.
3. Call 10 current clients from "host list" and ask for referral—goal is 5 names and #s.

EXPECTED HELP FROM COACH/ACTION STEPS:

Dry run on Naftaly presentation with me 4–4:30 Wed.
Call other regions to track down referral scripts by end of day Monday.

SALESPERSON SIGNATURE: COACH SIGNATURE:

MELISSA   KEVIN

Next Meeting Date: Time:
August 8, 2005   7:30

FIGURE 3.11   Goal-Setting Meeting

GSM Step 5: Encouragement

"Pretend that every single person you meet has a sign around his or her neck that says, 'Make me feel important.' Not only will you succeed in sales (or sales coaching), you will succeed in life."

—Mary Kay Ash, founder,
Mary Kay Cosmetics

"There are two things people want more than sex and money—recognition and praise."

—Mary Kay Ash

Based on the ideas from Mary Kay above, encouragement should come not only at the end of a GSM but throughout the meeting and throughout any of a coach's daily interactions. The truth is, just as Forrest Gump tells us, "Life [and a GSM] is like a box of chocolates. You never know what you're gonna get." GSMs can go smoothly, be very uncomfortable, become a career counseling session, or end up in a resignation. We hope that most of yours are positive and motivating for both coach and salesperson. Regardless of the tone of the GSM, there's never a reason why the coach should not end with positive encouragement. Here are a few examples:

- I believe in you.
- I can't wait to watch you succeed.
- I look forward to meeting with you again next month when you have blown away your goals.
- You're a real important part of this team. Thank you. I look forward to another great week from you.
- Go get 'em, tiger!

If the coach finds himself giving encouragement like, "I encourage you to work on your resume," the coaching relationship may not be moving in the right direction.

(AHS) Growing up in the Baltimore area, as an Oriole baseball fan in the 1970s, 1980s, and 1990s, we had a few years of excitement and many years of disappointment. I remained a fan through thick and thin, though. One particular year, when the O's were especially pitiful, I was still very excited to attend a certain game. My father had befriended the security guard who let the Oriole players in and out of the locker room, and he had invited my dad and me to stand outside the locker room before and after the game to meet some of the players. We arrived at the stadium very early, so that we could catch the Orioles on their way out to the field for batting practice. I brought a baseball with me so I would be prepared to get autographs. The Orioles started out on to the field one at a time, but getting autographs was not as easy as I expected. This was when the O's did not have many stars on the roster, and as the players passed me I did not recognize most of them, so I could not call them by name to stop them for an autograph. There was one player, however, that I knew I would recognize. Cal Ripken was the star of the team, and he had always been one of my heroes. So when Cal walked out, I perked up and asked: "Mr. Ripken, could I please have your autograph?" Sure enough, Cal stopped, asked my name, and I still have the ball: *Dear Adam, Best Wishes. Cal Ripken Jr.* I was obviously very excited.

My father and I went into the park and, since we still had a lot of time before it started, we sat in the bleachers to watch batting practice. I was pretty lucky that day because one of the members of the Milwaukee Brewers saw me in the bleachers and tossed a baseball up to me, so now I had two baseballs. The game went on and the Orioles lost by several runs, as usual, but I was not finished. I had a new ball now, and I wanted more autographs. After the game, as the Oriole players exited the locker room, it was even harder to recognize them because they were no longer in their uniforms but in street clothes. I knew I'd be able to recognize Cal Ripken again, and as an aspiring entrepreneur and collector of memorabilia, I wanted another autograph. Sure enough, Cal strolled out, and when I saw him I pulled out my new ball and said: "Good game, Cal. Can I please have an autograph?" As Cal leaned over to take my ball and pen he looked at me and snapped: "Hey. I remember you. You're Adam. You got my autograph before the game." And he walked off without signing the ball. How did that make me feel? Amazing! Cal Ripken, my hero, who signs thousands of autographs every week, remembered me! He made me feel important, and I've felt important ever since.

The point here is that the coach has a great opportunity to set up a very positive next GSM. By starting the next GSM with a review of last meeting's action steps and goals, the coach is communicating to the salesperson that she and her goals are very important to the coach and the team. Cal Ripken made me feel important when he remembered me three hours later. Imagine how well a coach can make his salespeople feel when he remembers what was important to them at last week's or month's goal-setting meeting. This is why most strong coaches will copy the documented GSM notes and make sure both parties have a copy to refer to between GSMs and at the next one.

Self-GSMs

Dale Carnegie, author of *How to Win Friends and Influence People*, calls *How I Raised Myself from Failure to Success in Selling*, by Frank Bettger, "the most helpful and inspiring book on salesmanship I have ever read." In the book Bettger, an insurance salesman who became one of the most successful and highly paid salesman in America, details how he succeeded in sales without the help of a regular coach or manager.

> Finally I got it through my head that I must take more time for planning. It was easy to throw forty or fifty prospect cards together and think I was prepared. That didn't take much time. But to go back over records, study each call carefully, plan exactly what I would say to each person, prepare proposals, write letters, and then make out a schedule, arranging each day's calls, Monday through Friday, in their proper order, required four to five solid hours of the most intensive kind of work.

Bettger did this "self-GSM" Saturday mornings until he eventually became efficient enough to do it Friday mornings. Bettger reviewed last week's calls, set next steps for prospects, then planned daily call routes and goals, and he documented everything. This process is very analogous to a salesperson working with his coach in a GSM to review last period's performance and set goals, action steps, and a game plan of attack for the upcoming period. Frank Bettger simply did GSMs on himself. He describes his results.

> Each Monday morning, when I started out, instead of having to drive myself to make calls, I walked in to see men with confidence and enthusiasm. I was eager and anxious to see them, because I had thought about them, studied their situation, and had some ideas I believed might be of value to them. At the end of the week, instead of

feeling exhausted and discouraged, I actually felt exhilarated and on fire with the excitement that next week I could do even better.

If you, like Frank Bettger, are not in a position with a regular sales coach, you too can perform self-GSMs to review last week, plan for next week, and be true to yourself with accountability. Figure 3.12 is an example of how you can fill out a goal-setting meeting documentation form on yourself.

GOAL-SETTING MEETING

SALESPERSON : MO   **DATE:** DECEMBER 3, 2005

REVIEW OF LAST MEETING ACTION STEPS:

Updated contact database by 12/1—done
Completed proposal for Tommy's—still need to work on pricing

Key Metric	Goal	Actual	+/–	New Goal
Cold Calls	100	115	+15	100
Cold Walking	5 hours	2 hours	-3	4 hours
Closed Deals	3	3	—	3

OBSERVATIONS:

I am great when I get my calls done each day between 8-10 AM. I know I will get my cold walking done this week because it is scheduled for 12/8 all afternoon. Closing that deal with Morgan's was huge. I know they can be a great referral source.

ACTION STEPS:

1. Complete Tommy's proposal and pricing on 12/5 for 12/7 presentation.
2. Attend Chamber meeting on 12/8 and practice elevator pitch in the car.
3. Order holiday thank you gifts on 12/9 for top customers.

SALESPERSON SIGNATURE: _MO_

Next Meeting Date: 12/10/03   Time: 8 AM

FIGURE 3.12 Goal-Setting Meeting

Other Best Practices on GSMs from Top Sales Teams

- Top performers tend to really appreciate the dedicated time to strategize with their coach. Everyone should look forward to these opportunities.
- Many coaches try to conduct all their GSMs on a specific planned day at the beginning of the week/month.
- Create a file to keep GSM documentation forms on each salesperson. This is a great way to catch trends and progress over time.
- When you set the next GSM you create an extra level of urgency to hit the goals and action steps, because a deadline now exists.
- Coaches and salespeople like the fact that GSMs force a dialogue on sales activity. Everyone is more successful this way.
- Some teams schedule GSMs back-to-back so that each one does not last too long.
- GSMs help with time management because they help to make sure salespeople are focused on the right activities, and they enable the coach to be more proactive with fewer fires to put out.
- Bring appointment calendars to GSMs so action steps can be set with documented deadlines.
- Schedule "coaching in the crunch" time during your GSMs.
- The coach's job is to get each salesperson to compete against his or her own potential. Top performers can still get better.
- The earlier in the day the GSM, the less likely it is to be rescheduled or put off.
- Some coaches schedule regular time in their day, week, and month to follow up on the goals and action steps set in GSMs.

Nice work! You made it through the GSM chapter. You are one step closer to being able to create a great salesperson in yourself or a teammate. In summary, we discussed the importance of GSMs and guidelines for administering them successfully. We outlined the process, then dug deeper into each step: Presenting the Agenda, Discovery, Solution and Game Plan, Summary and Commitment, and Encouragement. Along the way we learned and reviewed examples of key performance indicators, goal setting, pushing and pulling, SMART goals, and action steps. All along we emphasized the importance of proper documentation. Now that coach and salesperson have agreed upon a short term plan between GSMs, the coach-salesperson relationship enters a period in which the coach may need to transfer her skills to her salespeople. This happens through training, our topic in Chapter 4.

4 | Training

"I hated every minute of the training, but I said, 'Don't quit. Suffer now and live the rest of your life as a champion.'"

—Muhammad Ali, former
World Heavyweight Champion

Selling is everyone's business, and the largest room in the world is the room for self-improvement. We all can improve as salespeople, and one of the best ways to create a great salesperson, within yourself or others, is through training. Ideally, the sales coach is able to teach more of the skills required to become a great salesperson than the salespeople already know; or at least the coach has access to resources that can improve salespeople's skills and move them closer to greatness.

Let's review what has happened so far in previous chapters. The coach and salesperson have created, agreed upon, and committed to a business plan. Next, they began to participate in regular one-on-one GSMs to confirm that the salesperson is continuing to move toward the realization of her plan. Now, during a GSM (and/or through other forums that we will explain), the coach will begin to identify individual and team skill issues—see Figure 4.1.

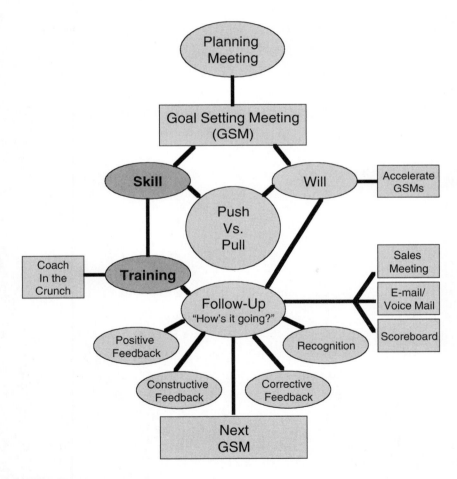

FIGURE 4.1   Coaching Model 4

These skill issues correspond to the gaps between the level salespeople are performing at now and the level at which top performing salespeople perform. Training is the best way to close this gap and develop the skills of a team or an individual.

If you are fortunate enough to have a coach, he may play the role of trainer, or you may have access to training from peers, an internal corporate training department, or the kind we like best—an external training partner. If you are an independent salesperson or entrepreneur, you may have to be creative in finding training resources. But there are plenty out there, including online training programs, seminars, consulting organizations/executive coaches, or informal mentors. Whether training comes from inside or outside your organization, and whether it comes from your supervisor or someone else, the best training, no matter from whom or how it is delivered, is that which is very regular and consistent. Skill building is not an easy process; it takes time, repetition, patience, and repetition.

The Coaching Model

(AHS) Before we launch into how the best coaches train, it is important to understand how people learn, because if learning does not happen, training will not be effective. To demonstrate the learning process, I will take you through some of the skill building that happened over several years in the early part of my life.

I grew up in Columbia, Maryland, between Baltimore and Washington, D.C., where the sport of lacrosse is quite popular. My father, Joel, grew up in the same area, and he has been involved with lacrosse during most of his life as a player, coach, fan, and referee. In fact, he has even been inducted into the Maryland Lacrosse Club Hall of Fame. Over the years, my father helped my brother, Jeff, and me learn lacrosse. We will use this context to explain how people move through the following stages of learning:

1. *Unconscious/Incompetent.* This is when you are not very good at doing something, and you don't know or care that you're not very good. Early in our lacrosse careers, my father bought Jeff and me lacrosse sticks. As young kids, we thought we were pretty cool because we each had our own sticks, just like our dad. Never mind that neither of us had any clue how to use a stick or actually play lacrosse. We would go out in the yard and try our best. We would throw the ball to one another and even catch it every now and then. We were pretty bad, but it didn't matter because we had no idea how bad we were.

2. *Conscious/Incompetent.* This is when you begin to realize that you are not good at something. As the years passed, Jeff and I became more interested in lacrosse. Our dad signed us up for youth leagues so we could continue to learn the sport with other kids. The real light bulb came on, though, when our dad started taking us to watch college lacrosse games. The college players were so big and strong and fast, and they never dropped the ball. These guys were amazing! Jeff and I would return home after the college games and try to practice all the moves we had just witnessed. We were not nearly as skilled as those college players, and we knew it. That "a-ha" moment was a good one for us, because it helped us realize what a great sport lacrosse was. Seeing the college

players perform motivated Jeff and me to practice so that we could one day be like them.

3. *Conscious/Competent.* This is when you start to improve your abilities and you are very aware of what you are doing as you build skills. As Jeff and I grew older, we started to play more and more organized lacrosse in middle school and through high school. We each became more comfortable with how to catch and throw and run the plays required to be successful in a game. As we grew as lacrosse players, Jeff and I were exposed to more and more coaches that helped us learn and build upon what our father had taught us.

4. *Unconscious/Competent.* This is when you have such strong skills in an area that you do not even need to think about what you are doing in order to execute at a high level. As Jeff and I finished high school we both had opportunities to play college lacrosse, Jeff at Ohio State and I at Cornell. When we stepped on the field in college, the teams we played with and against had very strong skills. We were now playing on the same fields where we had gained much of our initial inspiration and motivation to learn and practice lacrosse. The players were so highly skilled, and the action happened so fast, that there was never really any time to think about how to play. That was okay, however, because we had both been in so many lacrosse situations over the years—learning, practicing, and playing—that lacrosse was instinctive. We were unconsciously competent, which is the zone in which many top salespeople operate.

5. *Conscious/Competent Coach.* This is when someone who was once unconsciously competent needs to take a step back and consciously think through what has made him success-

ful so that he can teach the skills to others. Jeff and I didn't realize it, but our father had to become a conscious/competent coach to teach us the game after he had played so many years. Recently, Jeff and I have made this transition too. Now we are both washed up as players, but our friend Scott runs lacrosse camps and leagues for children. Occasionally, Scott will ask us to come to his events to help teach the kids about lacrosse. When Jeff and I go to the camps, we need to become very conscious again of all the little things that it takes to build skills. We need to carefully explain and give step-by-step demonstrations in order to really help our learners, the children, understand the new skills. We have to become conscious of the skills again, so that we can be competent coaches.

This last transition from unconscious/competent performer to conscious/competent coach is the most challenging. As a coach, or an experienced salesperson, you may have observed someone new and asked yourself: "What's wrong with that person? Why doesn't he just get it?" This is the struggle that many seasoned performers encounter when trying to become conscious again about the basics. This challenge is why many entrepreneurs, who are often great salespeople, have trouble increasing their businesses. They are unable to expand their organizations by increasing their scale through others because they cannot transfer their skills to others. There are only so many hours in a day that the leader can "do the job." Many sales organizations promote their best salespeople into management with hopes that these top performing salespeople can teach an entire team of salespeople what worked well for them. Some make this transition successfully, others do not. Sales coaches often do not have enough hours to do the job for all their salespeople. While the product knowledge may be similar, it is critical to acknowledge the fact that teaching the job requires a very different skill set from doing the job.

As we are writing this book, Wayne Gretzky has just accepted the challenging job of coaching the Phoenix Coyotes hockey team. Hockey fans consider Gretzky to be one of the top players of all time; he is called "The Great One." The Great One as a player, that is. It will be interesting to watch how well Gretzky fares in his efforts to train his team and become the conscious/competent coach.

What is training? Training is one's ability to close that last gap and become a conscious/competent coach, after having performed at an unconscious/competent level. In order to transfer skills to someone else, the coach must consciously understand the skills behind what he does, then follow a disciplined and repetitive process to aid someone else in gaining those same skills. It doesn't sound easy, does it? It's not. Here are some of the challenges of training:

- Training takes time. Most businesses, especially within the sales organizations, need results now if not yesterday. Training requires a significant long-term time investment that can mean sacrificing short-term results. If a coach feels the need to produce quickly, he may err on the side of doing the job for the salesperson, instead of the slower process of teaching the salesperson to do the job herself. If it's January and the coach does the job for the new salesperson, the team may sell more in January. But if in January the coach spends time training the new salesperson to do the job, the team may sell

less in January but more in February, March, April, and all
the other months this year and in years to come.

- Some coaches do not know how to train. This chapter is de-
  signed to fix that. One of the most common "training" techniques is for a coach to take a salesperson on a call, have the
  salesperson observe the coach once, and then let the salesperson loose into the world with a pat on the back: "Okay,
  now it's your turn. Go make it happen. It's that easy." The
  salesperson has no idea how to "make it happen" because he
  is consciously incompetent and all he's done is observe an
  unconsciously competent performance, which is very difficult to duplicate. Other coaches will train via the "Read this
  manual—it has everything you need to know" approach. Or
  worse, the "Go out there and make calls—you'll figure it
  out" approach. There are salespeople who were able to succeed with these types of "training," but they are few and far
  between.

- All of the tools and resources may not be available. With
  many salespeople working in remote and distant territories
  from where their coaches work, they share very little face-
  to-face time in which training can occur. Additionally, with
  technology changing so rapidly, some companies introduce
  new products and services so often that there is no time to
  train on them.

- Coaches who are strong trainers possess an extraordinary
  amount of persistence and patience, which are not easy traits
  to develop. As Kevin Morrissey, Vice President of Fleet Services at Enterprise Rent-A-Car puts it, "I believe a coach
  needs a relentless appetite for repetition." For example, many

people say the opening three minutes of a sales call can make or break the call and can be very important to the ultimate relationship or lack thereof. Accordingly, a sales coach could easily practice and rehearse those opening three minutes 10 to 20 times with a new salesperson and be very effective as a trainer. Such a practice session will take 30 to 60 minutes, and the coach will have covered only the first three minutes of what to do in a sales call, with a lot more to practice. Incidentally, this is why most coaches practice a skill like this only once or twice, which we believe is not nearly enough. The point is, to be an effective trainer and coach, you will often be doing something that you may have done thousands of times before. This repetition takes a great deal of patience, which is not easy.

- Training can be expensive. Depending on how training is conducted, you may be dealing with travel expenses, consulting fees, and almost certainly time out of production (which we promise coaches will hear about from salespeople). We are confident that, when executed properly, the investment is worth every penny and then some.

- Training requires getting people out of their comfort zones. This includes the salesperson and the trainer/coach. Training needs to be lively and interactive, whether in a group setting or one-on-one. This interactivity requires practice aloud, which requires expanding our comfort zones. Insanity has been defined as, "doing the same thing over and over again, the way you've always done it, and expecting a different result." If you want to improve as a coach or as a salesperson, you must expand your comfort zone, which is not easy. Human beings get used to staying within their comfort zones; they also get used to being mediocre. If you want to be exceptional, do something outside your comfort zone every day.

Which of the foregoing challenges sound most familiar to you?

(AHS) When I was relatively new at The Next Level, late in my first month on the job, I was excited about the first day in which I would be using the phone to arrange appointments to potentially sell our consulting services. I had made thousands of telephone sales calls in other sales organizations and always enjoyed it, so I was excited to try it in this business. I got into the office early that morning, feeling ready to go. The goal that my sales coach and I had talked about was to make 100 dials in my first day of telephone prospecting. I walked into my sales coach's office and said, "OK, I'm ready to dial. Who do I call?" "No problem," my sales coach said as he handed me a list of names and numbers of sales executives in our target market. I turned back to walk toward my phone and then I thought of another challenge: "What do I say when someone answers?" "No problem," my sales coach said, and this time he handed me a phone script that had worked for other salespeople in our organization. Again I turned around and headed toward my phone, then thought of another challenge: "But what do I say if they have questions for me that I can't answer?" "Look, Adam. You're going to make 100 dials today! I don't care if you dial the phone 100 times and say 'Hello this is Adam from the Next Level—BOO!' and hang up the phone. You're going to get to 100!" And off I went.

In this instance, my sales coach may not have been as patient a trainer as he could have been, but he did teach me a very helpful lesson with regard to repetition. My coach was not worried about my skills at that point. He just wanted me to get my feet wet and do the job repeatedly. I did make 100 dials that day (and did not have to use the BOO! line once), made eleven contacts, and set two appointments (versus my goal of one), one with an executive at a financial services firm and one with a contact in the medical devices industry. Years later, I still know that I can improve my telephone prospecting skills—training takes time.

Now that we have presented all the reasons that training is challenging to execute properly, we will explain the reasons behind the training—the benefits that outweigh all of the challenges. After all, the more you learn, the more you earn!

Benefits of Training

- When training is conducted in a group setting, it creates a positive, solution-focused winning environment. It fosters camaraderie within the team and builds a better team for the long run.
- When training is done right, people's skills improve. Skill building has an infinite amount of associated benefits, including many of the others on this list.
- When skills improve through training, confidence also improves among salespeople. Confidence is a hugely beneficial attribute that most top performing salespeople and sales

coaches possess. It does not matter if a customer is purchasing a $2 toothbrush or a $2 million home, customers want confidence from salespeople. Think about how you felt after your last training experience. Did you come out ready to take on the world?

- Training creates enthusiasm in individuals and within the team. Enthusiasm is the little recognized secret to success. The more salespeople we meet, the more we are convinced that enthusiasm is integral to many top performers' successes. This sincerity and the ability to get excited about what you are selling can be a direct result of the right kind of training.

- When people build skills through training, their performance potential grows. As people stay motivated to achieve their potentials and set big goals during GSMs, results improve, and everyone is happier with more sales and higher profits.

- Training improves morale and employee retention. When people feel that the company is interested in investing time and money in them, they feel good about their jobs. Also, since effective training helps salespeople and coaches perform well and succeed, people stay longer because they are winning.

Training is tough, but you should still do it. Here are some of the opportunities or forums during which training can happen:

- *Business planning meeting.* During the business planning meeting a coach may need to train salespeople on how to create a plan. This is a good opportunity to share examples and tell stories of other successful salespeople and how they started off their years with the same type of plan.

- *Goal-setting meeting.* During a GSM, through proper dis-covery, a coach will often identify a particular skill issue. For example, if a telephone salesperson has a high number of dials but has not contacted a high percentage of deci-sion-makers, she may be having trouble getting past the gatekeeper. A good coach could identify this issue through proper questioning. If there is enough time during the GSM, it may be appropriate to train on the opening line so that the salesperson can build skills and confidence in that area immediately.

- *A scheduled one-on-one training session.* At times, a coach may identify a certain skill issue and may not be able to address it immediately. In this case, time should be scheduled to con-centrate on the issue. For example, if a salesperson and coach decide to go through a dry run of a customer presentation, they may schedule a separate meeting to do so.

- *Coaching in the crunch.* Training opportunities often arise while coaches are out in the field, or side-by-side in the of-fice performing the steps of a sales call or presentation with the salespeople. The training typically happens immediately before or after the customer interaction. For example, we see many top coaches practicing pieces of a meeting in the car with a salesperson on the way to the meeting.

- *In team meetings.* Some coaches include training in every reg-ular sales meeting, while others schedule separate group training sessions. This is often most relevant when coaches notice that several team members could all benefit from training on a similar issue. Training in a group setting is great for team building and creates lots of opportunities for public recognition.

- *Spontaneous opportunities.* The best sales coaches always have their training hats on. While walking around the office, they will hear a salesperson on the phone. After the call, the coach can immediately train the salesperson on how to improve a certain portion of the call. This quick training is excellent because often the salesperson has an opportunity to implement it and see success with the training immediately.

Great coaches understand the benefits of training, are able to overcome the challenges in training, and also capitalize on all the ideal opportunities to transfer their skills to others. Additional characteristics we have noticed in top performing training coaches are:

- Willingness and dedication to training preparation. These coaches prepare for a training session the way top salespeople prepare for a big sales call. They review the material, put together an agenda, and identify clear goals and training objectives. They do not just show up for a training event and wing it.
- Patience, persistence, and tolerance for repetition. Strong coaches figure out what works and then teach it over and over again on the same audiences and eventually on new audiences. "What works" does not change much, so what's old and easy for the coach needs to be delivered in a fashion that's new, exciting, and challenging.

- High level of competence in the skills they are training on. Top coaches make sure they are bulletproof in the skills on which they will be teaching. Training is a great opportunity to demonstrate, build trust, and establish that "street cred" that all salespeople expect in their coach. It is also an opportunity to damage trust and "street cred" if the coach does not demonstrate the skills well. This goes back to the first point of making sure the coach is well prepared before the training begins.
- Confidence and belief in their audience. The best trainers deliver their message with conviction and confidence in the material and in their audience's ability to succeed by using the material. Their attitude is, "I know this stuff works, and I know you can make it work well for you!" Salespeople can sense this attitude and appreciate the vote of confidence from their coach.

How do you train? What does the coach say and do? How can the coach most efficiently and effectively transfer her skills to someone else? Of the 10,000 coaches we have worked with, we have found that the top performers follow a training process like the one shown in Figure 4.2.

The Training Process

Top coaches first explain the skill they are about to teach, highlight why it is important, and tell when the skill is applicable. Then they give a top-notch demonstration. After that they practice back

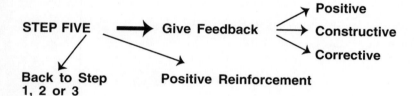

STEP ONE ➡ **Explain**

STEP TWO ➡ **Demonstrate**

STEP THREE ➡ **Practice with Coaching**

STEP FOUR ➡ **Observe/Listen**

STEP FIVE ➡ **Give Feedback** ⟨ **Positive**
                                          Constructive
                                          Corrective

Back to Step   **Positive Reinforcement**
1, 2 or 3

FIGURE 4.2   The Training Process

and forth with the salespeople several times, allowing them to observe each other. Finally, the coach gives appropriate feedback based on the practice session. The largest gap we see between coaches that are great trainers and all others is that the great ones show and tell; all the others just tell. Instead of "do it like this," top coaches say, "Watch me do it like this, so that you really know what 'like this' means."

The following training process can be used whether you are teaching someone to bake a cake, do aerobics, or make a cold call. The sequence is not necessarily always chronological in order; rather, it is a fluid process that requires coaches to adapt to the needs of the audience. We will break down each step of the process so that you can take a methodical and successful approach to training.

Step 1: Explain

Coaches must first explain the skill they are about to transfer. Explaining the skill helps the audience understand when and how the skill will be applicable, which should generate some enthusiasm for learning. Great salespeople love learning new skills or practicing old skills that will help them sell more. The specific technique used to explain a new skill is to highlight what, why, and how for the training exercise. Here's an example:

> [*What*] We are about to learn cold calling techniques that you can use to get past the gatekeeper. [*Why*] This will help you make more contacts over the phone each day, which will lead to more appointments and more sales. [*How*] First I'll review a technique and a script and practice it on you as the gatekeeper. Then we will reverse roles several times until you feel very comfortable. Then you can swing into action and use these gatekeeper techniques on the phone today.

This very thorough explanation sets the stage for the training process and is a natural transition to step two, the coach's demonstration.

Step 2: Demonstrate

There is a legendary story (related to us by our friend and mentor Earl Taylor) that goes like this: Every year at the state fair, there is a contest to see who has raised the biggest stud bull. One particular cattleman won and put his bull in a tent with the trophy by it and the big blue ribbon on it and began to charge everybody who wanted to see the bull 25 cents. This became very profitable. A man walks in and asks to see if there is a discount to see the bull as he has a very large family. The cattleman denies him. The man looks at his family and decides to give it another try. "Please, I have a large family. We have driven a long way. Is there anything you can do?" He appeals to the cattleman so the cattleman asks, "How many kids do you have?" The man says, "I have 23." The cattleman, thinking like a cattleman, says to himself. "Man, this guy is a great producer!" He says, "How many kids do you have with you?" The man says 17. The cattleman says, "I will let you, your wife, and all 17 of your kids come in at once, but you have to be all together." The man is overjoyed and says, "That's great, but why are you being so nice to us?" The cattleman says, "I want you and your family to see my bull. Even more important than that, I want my bull to see you!"

So if a good demonstration is important to training from father to bull; it is probably a key step in training from coach to salesperson.

The demonstration step of the skill development process is critical because research shows that people learn only 16 percent of what they read; 20 percent of what they see (demonstration); 30 percent of what they are told (explanation); 50 percent of what they see and are told (explanation and demonstration); and 90 percent of what they do (explain, demonstrate, and practice). The practice obviously comes after the demonstration, but the quality of the practice session is directly related to the quality of the coach's demonstration. The demonstration sets the bar, so the salesperson will typically only be as strong as the coach, at best.

A strong demonstration is also key because it is a great opportunity for the coach to build credibility with her people. Establishing this "street cred" is essential in opening lines of communication and it successfully tees up future training opportunities. In other words, if salespeople see their coach in action and think, "She's really good at this stuff. I'd like to be as strong as she is one day," they become open to feedback and training from the coach. The alternative—salespeople see their coach in action and think, "She's not any better than I am anyway," or, "She doesn't really know what it's like with real prospects and clients"—creates a situation in which the salespeople will not be nearly as receptive to future feedback and training sessions.

Legendary UCLA basketball coach John Wooden highlights the importance of demonstrating the basics, even with his top-tier college athletes:

> Over the years I have become convinced that every detail is important and that success usually accompanies attention to little details. It is this, in my judgment, that makes for the difference between champion and near champion.
>
> One of the little things I watch closely is a player's socks. No basketball player is better than his feet. If they hurt, if his shoes don't fit, or if he has blisters, he can't play the game. It is amazing how few players know how to put on a pair of socks properly. I don't want blisters, so each year I give in minute detail a step-by-step *demonstration* as to precisely how I want them to put on their socks, every time. Believe it or not, there's an art to doing it right, and it makes a big difference in the way a player's feet stand the

pounding of practice and the game. Wrinkles which cause blisters can be eliminated by just a little attention.

Along this same line, I attach great importance to the shoes our players wear and how they fit. When most of them come to us, they are wearing shoes a size to a size-and-a-half too large. This seems to be a holdover from childhood, but our players' feet aren't going to grow much. If they do, we'll resize them with new shoes. I want the toe of the foot to be exactly at the end of the shoe when they are standing up so that when they make a quick stop, the foot won't slide."

If John Wooden can demonstrate, in training his championship athletes, fundamentals like how to put on socks and wear properly sized shoes, can't all of us demonstrate and practice the important fundamentals of our jobs? The best coaches and salespeople execute flawless and consistent demonstrations and practice the basics.

Step 3: Practice with Coaching

"Champions keep playing until they get it right."
　　　　　—Billie Jean King, American tennis
　　　　　champion, first female athlete
　　　　　to earn $100,000 in one year

Repetitive practice is probably the most simple step of the training process—coach demonstrates, then salesperson makes an attempt, then coach redemonstrates, then salesperson tries again—over and over. It is the most challenging step because it is monotonous and requires a tremendous amount of patience from the coach and salesperson.

In the movie *Miracle*, the 1980 United States Olympic men's hockey team pulls off the "miracle on ice" by defeating the highly favored Russians, and then going on to win the gold medal. Prior to the Olympics, the team's legendary coach, Herb Brooks, had a particularly memorable experience with his new team. After a preliminary hockey game, in which Brooks did not feel that the team played to its potential, the coach had all his players return to the ice in the dark, empty rink. He had the team skate sprints over and over for a long period. Every time the team returned to the starting line, Brooks simply blew the whistle and repeated one word: "Again!" And the team took off down the ice again. This experience turned into a tremendous team-building session and emphasized the importance of repetitive practice in a championship team.

If you, as a coach or a salesperson, are ever uncertain as to whether you should continue practicing a certain skill, just think back to *Miracle* and Herb Brooks and practice "again."

Some salespeople love training and practicing new skills. These folks are great to work with whether you are their coach or peer. Every now and then, you will come across people who say, "I hate role-playing. It's not real anyway." We agree with the idea that it can be challenging to replicate during a practice session exactly how things will happen with a real prospect or client. However, what we think is "not real" is when a salesperson heads into a sales opportunity unrehearsed, without having practiced several times. In this scenario, the salesperson is nervous, doesn't listen well (because he has to think about what he's going to say next), and is unable to be "real" himself.

People say they don't like role-playing because it gets them out of their comfort zones, which is exactly what is required to improve. Observing top performers in other fields illustrates this point: Will Ferrell practiced being "Frank the Tank" numerous times before filming *Old School*; Kenny Chesney, the 2005 Academy of Country Music Entertainer of the Year, practiced singing "When the Sun Goes Down" hundreds of times with Uncle Cracker before performing for a live audience; and the New England Patriots practiced their plays thousands of times before they won the Super Bowl. Just as with a prospect or client, the Patriots did not know exactly how their opponent would respond to certain plays, but they knew that if they practiced enough so that they could execute them without thinking, they would be able to think about how to adjust or customize the plays to each opponent.

We find that salespeople generally fall into the following three categories with respect to their approach toward training and improving:

The Growth Zone. This is where people learn most easily. They are open-minded and very receptive. They know they must get out of their comfort zones to achieve the desired results from the training. Are you in the growth zone when you attend trainings? Who on your sales team is always in the growth zone? How do they maintain this open attitude?

The End Zone. This is when people are too good to practice. They have it all figured out in their own minds, but are often not nearly as strong as they think they are. Do you have anyone on your team that has always "been there or done that?" Are they often not as credible as they think they are?

The Dead Zone. This is when people have no active interest in learning or improving. People in the dead zone never try new concepts. They have been in sales for over 20 years with only one year of sales experience. Do you have people in the dead zone on your team? How can you fix or replace them?

It is important to be aware of the zones whether you are a coach or a salesperson. We spend a lot of time training individuals and groups in our jobs as consultants. (AHS) Early on in my career, when I would come across people in the end zone or dead zone, I would go way out of the way in an effort to get them to participate more than they wanted to. In doing so, I would take my time and energy away from those who were in the growth zone. I then realized that I shouldn't be spending my time with the people who do not want it. Our advice is to coach and train the people who want to be coached and trained, and everyone will be happier.

If you are a salesperson, it is important to be aware of these zones so that you can prepare your attitude and embrace training opportunities by positioning yourself in the growth zone.

To be clear with what actually happens in the "Practice with Coaching" step: After the coach's demonstration(s), the salesperson has an opportunity to practice the skill on the coach. You repeat the process several times. The coach must be sensitive about the "coaching" portion in this stage. Top coaches seem to start off by highlighting only the positives during the first few repetitions, which should build the salesperson's confidence. As confidence builds, the coach can become increasingly more critical in the coaching feedback.

Step 4: Observe/Listen

The observe step really happens throughout the entire training process, with each party observing the other.

A few years ago Chris Mullin, former National Basketball Association superstar, was approached by a colleague for some help. This other player had attended St. Johns University, as did Mullin, so they shared a common bond. The other man was also quite successful as a player, and he too went on to become an NBA All-Star. At this point in his career, however, the player was having a very tough time shooting free throws. So he contacted Mullin, one of the best free throw shooters ever, to see if he would be willing to give him some advice and coaching. The player offered to pay Mullin whatever he wanted. Mullin agreed happily, said he'd help, and that the only thing he expected in return was a couple of cheeseburgers. The two met at a gym and Mullin grabbed a ball and told the player to "observe" him. The other player sat there and "observed" as Chris Mullin shot and made 200 consecutive free throws. Then he turned to his peer and explained that the way to get better at free throws is to shoot them, over and over again. Mullin gave a very impressive demonstration and sent a strong message by having his peer observe him.

As the salesperson observes the coach practicing, he should try to watch for behaviors that he can copy. As the coach observes, she should think about which steps in the training process the team may need to revisit. Is more explanation required? Does the salesperson need another demonstration? Should we continue to practice more?

Step 5: Feedback

During the training process and practice sessions, one of the best ways for a coach to continue to build confidence and competence within a salesperson is with proper feedback. Feedback is the greatest motivator of people, especially when it is immediate, which it should be within a training session. For example, when you touch a hot stove, the immediate feedback is the burning sensation on your skin, so you are quickly motivated to move. When you make a big sale, your immediate feedback is the pride and satisfaction you feel, so you are motivated to make your next big sale. Here we will discuss the three types of feedback—positive, constructive, and corrective—within the training context. We will expand further into this topic in subsequent chapters.

Positive Feedback. Positive feedback is easy to give and absolutely invaluable. It costs nothing to deliver, other than a few seconds, and the return on that tiny investment is often too large to measure. Positive feedback in a training interaction is when the coach recognizes something that the salesperson says or does particularly well or when the coach simply thanks the salesperson for his or her effort in trying to improve. It is critical that this feedback be delivered with a genuine tone.

For example, when I was first learning how to sell our consulting services at The Next Level, Steve Johnson taught me how to explain product knowledge using features, bridges, and benefits. During several portions of the training, Steve delivered positive reinforcement like this:

> *Steve:* Adam, your enthusiasm during our practice sessions has been excellent today! If you are that excited when speaking to our prospects and clients about The Next Level, you will be sure to get them very excited as well. You're going to sell a lot of business if you keep that up. I really appreciate your effort.
>
> *Adam:* Thanks! I feel great today. I guess I'm just feelin' it!

Great coaches are always looking for opportunities to deliver positive feedback, within or outside of training sessions, because they know it helps to inspire superior performance and makes people feel great.

Constructive Feedback. Constructive feedback is when the coach acknowledges what the salesperson does well in the training session and offers suggestions on how to improve the quality of the performance. For example, in my same training experience with Steve, I remember the following discussion:

> *Steve:* Adam, your explanation of the features and benefits was really well done. I liked the way you mentioned that "We've been in business for over ten years, which means we are stable as a business partner." That will really help us build credibility with new prospects. One thing you can add to that presentation is simply using the word 'you' with a bridge that makes sure you highlight the benefit from the prospect's perspective. It would sound like this: "We've been in business for over ten years and the benefit to you is that we are stable as a business partner." Does that make sense?
>
> *Adam:* It really does. Now I see why you've been so successful. That feedback was well delivered. You must have read *Selling Is Everyone's Business.* I feel very motivated right now. Can we practice more?

When constructive feedback is delivered properly in a training context, both coach and salesperson feel sure that progress is being made and their time together is helping to improve skills and, ultimately, performance.

Corrective Feedback. Corrective feedback in a training session is when the coach needs to redirect the performance of the salesperson because the salesperson is considerably off track. Early in that same training session with Steve, I received some corrective feedback:

> *Steve:* Adam. In your practice presentation, when you highlighted what we offer at The Next Level, you mentioned lots of features, such as that we've been in business for over ten years and that we focus on best practices. It is also important that you highlight the related benefits to our clients, because that is what people really buy. For example, you could have pointed out how the ten years of experience gives our clients peace of mind with respect to our credibility and stability. Or you can mention that because we focus on industry and company top performer best practices, our clients find that our solutions are extremely relevant. Do you see the difference?
>
> *Adam:* I see. I need to remember to point out what's in it for them. Let me practice again.

In training, when the coach delivers corrective feedback, he will often provide additional explaining and demonstrating. Any feedback, regardless of how positive or critical, should leave the salesperson feeling motivated. If the salesperson is doing the right things, she should receive feedback that motivates her to do more of them. If the salesperson needs some adjustment to her performance, she should receive feedback that motivates her to change and improve her performance. Keeping feedback and the overall training interaction motivating is not always easy, but it is crucial because it makes the training experience fun for everyone. This is key when a coach is trying to instill a culture of continuous improvement, as top coaches do.

An important question for both coaches and salespeople to consider with respect to the training process is, "How do we know whether or not the training worked?" Simply put, when a salesperson can effectively execute the skill being trained, without the coach being there, the training has been successful.

Self-Directed Training

If you are a salesperson who does not have a large corporate infrastructure or a formal sales coach to rely on for training, fear not. We have seen many people be very successful on their own with self-directed training via the following:

- They seek out their own informal mentors.
- They take classes in their communities.
- They read books.
- They subscribe to publications and read articles.
- They go to seminars.
- They listen to CDs or tapes in their cars.
- They join associations or other networking groups.

These approaches obviously require significant discipline and initiative, but that's what it takes to be successful in sales, especially if you expect to continue to improve throughout your career.

Summary

To summarize this chapter, we began with how people learn, and then we identified the challenging transition from unconscious/competent performer to conscious/competent coach. Then we defined training and discussed relevant challenges, benefits, and opportunities that come with training. Finally, we delved into the specifics of the training process with these five steps: Explain, Demonstrate, Practice with Coaching, Observe, and Give Feedback.

Overall, in our efforts to create a great salesperson, we have hit on the importance of coaching, GSMs, and now training. Next is follow-up, during which coaches check in on goals, action steps, and skills regularly throughout the week or month.

5 | Follow-Up— "How's It Going?"

A 12-year-old red-headed boy named Mel lived in a small town. One day, as he rode his shiny, new, red bike down Main Street, he decided to pull over and go to the ice cream parlor. He walked to the back of the parlor and found the gentleman who owned the establishment. Mel asked softly, in his young voice, "Could I please borrow your telephone to make a call?" The owner reluctantly agreed and handed Mel the phone. He dialed a number and the conversation went like this:

Mrs. Brown: Brown residence.
Mel: Good afternoon, Mrs. Brown. I was riding my bike past your lawn today and noticed that you have one of the nicest lawns in the whole town. I cut people's lawns in town to earn some money. Would you be interested in letting me cut your lawn?

Mrs. Brown: Thank you for the compliment and for the offer. But we already have a nice young man who cuts our lawn.

Mel: But when I cut people's lawns, I mow one week north-south, and the next week east-west, so the blades of grass stand straight up all year long.

Mrs. Brown: That's a very nice offer, but the boy who cuts our lawn already does that.

Mel: And when I cut lawns, I rake up all the grass clippings so your lawn will look beautiful when I'm finished.

Mrs. Brown: I bet you do. I'm sorry to tell you that the young man who cuts our lawn provides that service too, but thank you.

Mel: But Mrs. Brown, I have a special edger that I use to trim the edges of your lawn around the sidewalk and walkways, so your lawn will look perfect when I'm finished.

Mrs. Brown: You know, the little boy that does our lawn provides that service for us too.

Mel: Okay, Mrs. Brown. What if I could provide you with all of these great services, but at a lower price than you are currently paying?

Mrs. Brown: The boy who cuts our lawn has never raised his price on us in two years. My husband and I were just considering giving him a raise.

Mel: Okay, I understand. Best of luck with your lawn.

And the boy hung up the phone. As he handed it back to the parlor owner, the older gentleman complimented the young man: "I have to hand it to you, young man. I was listening to you on that call. You were really enthusiastic and persistent. If you keep that up, you're going to be cutting a lot of lawns in this town. And I bet one day, you'll even cut that Mrs. Brown's lawn." To which Mel replied, "I already cut her lawn. I just wanted to see how I was doing."

In the same way that Mel followed up with his client, it is important for coaches to follow up on the commitments that salespeople make. Now we will return to the coaching model (see Figure 5.1) and our efforts to create a great salesperson. At this point, the duo has completed the business plan, which happens once a year and is referred to regularly throughout the year. (Some coaches and salespeople conduct an additional meeting midyear to update the business plan.) Then the duo meets monthly or weekly in a GSM to review performance and construct short-term game plans that align with the business plan. During these meetings and through other opportunities, the coach will identify certain skill issues and conduct training to address the needs. In the business plan there are yearly goals, in the GSMs there are monthly or weekly action steps, and there are often regular skill areas to check on after training sessions. The best coaches do not wait for the next event or meeting to do their checking. Instead, they follow up spontaneously and regularly, asking the question, "How's it going?" to check the status of goals, action steps, and skill areas. We will discuss the specific applications of asking "How's it going?" later in this chapter.

The Coaching Model

Lance Armstrong, the seven-time Tour de France champion and cancer survivor, has said, "I'm a believer in momentum." While setting goals during a meeting and writing them down is a significant

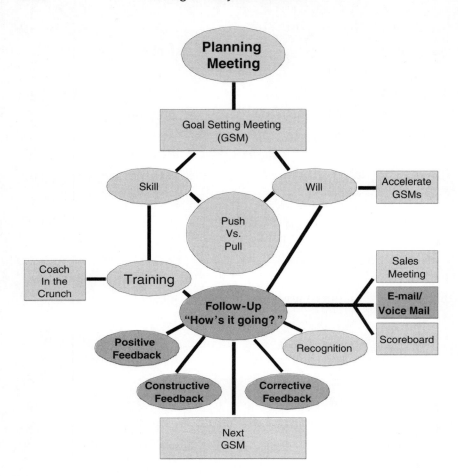

FIGURE 5.1   Coaching Model 5

step toward being successful in sales, in order to make sure goals are being worked on the best coaches capitalize on the momentum that begins with business planning and GSMs; then they build on that momentum by following up with feedback hourly, daily, and weekly.

A *Fortune* magazine article titled, "Why CEOs Fail" reports that 70 percent of executive failures are due to poor execution. The article notes, "It's bad execution. As simple as that: not getting things done, being indecisive, not delivering on commitments. We base our conclusions on careful study of several dozen CEO failures we've observed over the decades. . . . The results are beyond doubt." The article also states, "It's clear, as well, that getting execution right will only become more crucial." We bring this point to your attention because we know the best way to execute as a coach is to make sure your people execute, and the best way to make sure they execute is to follow up on the most important priorities.

For the purposes of this book, we are defining follow-up as all the regular, informal opportunities to reinforce the expectations in the business plan and the goals and actions steps set in GSMs. Follow-up is the coach's way of ensuring that the regular activities the salespeople are engaged in are in line with what both parties agreed to in the business plan and the GSMs. The advantage to having a vision and incremental goals to support that vision within your business plan is that you can ask yourself this fairly honest question at any point: "Is what I'm doing right now helping me to move closer to my ultimate vision and helping me meet my goals?"

An example of someone who illustrates this point is our friend Naft. Naft's vision for the year is to increase his sales by 20 percent, and one of the monthly goals that support his vision is to generate five new qualified prospects each month by asking current clients for referrals. If Naft is at his desk calling clients, gauging their level of satisfaction and asking for referrals, his current activity is in line with his plan and he can answer "yes" to the question above. If Naft is at his desk reviewing his fantasy football injury report on the Internet, his current activity is probably not in line with his vision and goals. He would probably answer "no" to the above question.

Lou, a very successful manager at a financial services firm, understands the importance of follow-up: "Follow-up is critical, especially when you are coaching a team. It is important to get around every day and say 'good morning' to the salespeople as well as to the staff. Ask: 'How are you feeling?' 'How was your weekend?' This little conversation goes a long way—they know you are interested in them and they feel comfortable sharing their successes and challenges. Following up like this is a great opportunity to praise yesterday's performance. And if you're not walking around, you become an absentee manager, just an authoritative figure in the corner, versus a business partner." Here are some of the other benefits of effective, regular follow-up:

- Follow-up creates a consistent message and focus. These sporadic interactions are great opportunities to reinforce the message from business plans, GSMs, training sessions, time spent "coaching in the crunch" in the field with salespeople, and sales meetings or huddles.
- Spending time following up creates more coaching opportunities through "coachable moments." Coaches help salespeople sell more. If they don't, they shouldn't be there. Accordingly, observing techniques and following up on objectives means that coach and salesperson spend more time together, which, in turn, means more growth opportunities

and higher sales. This is just one more opportunity for a coach to identify and solve skill or will issues.

- Regular follow-up impacts performance immediately. It's fine to check in at a formal, documented GSM weekly or monthly, but people can get off track between meetings. It is human nature to become distracted. If a salesperson is off track and not working effectively toward goals, it is in the best interest of both the salesperson and the coach to have that salesperson redirected as soon as possible. It works the same way when a salesperson is on the right track. Hearing positive reinforcement from the coach ensures that the salesperson will continue down that right track, while building confidence and momentum in that salesperson.

- Great salespeople appreciate follow-up. This is one of the coach's most effective methods to demonstrate to the salespeople that he cares. When a coach follows up, he is taking a genuine interest in his salesperson's success. Most coaches are very knowledgeable and have the capacity to help the people on their teams. In order to follow up with feedback that is received with an open mind, however, coaches need to establish trust. As Nick Murray, one of the financial service industry's most popular speakers and writers, says in *The Excellent Investment Advisor*, "People do not begin to care what you know until they begin to know that you care."

It's important to remember a concept that we reviewed in the GSM chapter. This regular and consistent follow-up works best when there are very specific, previously agreed upon, goals and action steps. For example, I can pass Anna's desk and ask her, "How's the prospecting going?" Or if Anna and I have already agreed on a clear and specific goal, I can ask, "How are you doing on the goal to get 50 calls in by 10 A.M.?" The second approach shows Anna that I care enough about her to remember her specific goal and gives me the opportunity to play my part in helping her hit it. The first approach is better than nothing, but it is not specific to Anna or her plan. "How's the prospecting going?" is a generic question that is relevant to almost any salesperson.

In some instances salespeople or coaches who implement very specific or more consistent approaches to follow-up can be perceived as being micromanagers. Ineffective management or micromanagement (not one and the same) occurs when there is not an agreed upon plan in place and there are no specific goals and action steps set. In these cases the coach has no insight or control over the salespeople's game plan or daily activities. The coach feels the need to try to gain more control, and often becomes overbearing with questions like, "What are you doing today? Why are you doing that right now? What are you doing next?" This is micromanagement and it frustrates salespeople. Coaches only need to ask these questions in the absence of specific goals and action steps. The most successful coaches follow up with their salespeople in specific terms and with frequency, but are not perceived as micromanagers. They ask specific follow-up questions to help salespeople stay accountable to their specific goals. This method sets up a dynamic of support and advocacy, not one of spying and skepticism.

The major difference between a coach who demonstrates effective follow-up and one who micromanagers is based on what happens before the follow-up takes place. If there is already a clear agenda to follow up on (set during a GSM or in a business plan), then the follow-up and feedback should be motivating for both the coach and salesperson. Keep in mind, great coaches do not only follow up when something is wrong. In fact, the whole reason they are able to correct improper behavior is that they have built a trustful relationship through the development of open dialogue, constant feedback, and recognition when people do things right. Follow-up must be regular and consistent during all times: the good, the bad, and the ugly. If follow up is used only to correct actions when a coach sees a salesperson doing the wrong thing, an adversarial relationship arises. Salespeople hide from their coach out of fear because they know every interaction is going to be negative. This sets up a dishonest relationship in which salespeople avoid their coach. It would have been challenging for Phil Jackson to win nine National Basketball Association championships as a coach if all of his players hid inside their lockers at game time.

The coaching model diagram highlights voice mail and e-mail as effective means for follow-up. We have seen some coaches use these means of communication effectively and some use them poorly. Some salespeople and coaches work at long distances from one another, and many people in sales work in the early mornings and late evenings, so face-to-face or voice-to-voice contact is not always possible. E-mail and voice mail are practical modes for providing follow-up and feedback when recognizing and rewarding the right behaviors. However, in e-mail, it is difficult to incorporate tone into correspondence, and often the proper context is missing. This can lead to misunderstanding. Here's an example of an effective follow-up e-mail from coach to salesperson:

Dorothy—
I looked at last night's performance report. Great job closing that ACME deal yesterday! I know you've been working hard on that. Keep up the nice work this month and you'll blow out your business

plan goal of three new accounts per month. How many do you think
you can get this month?

This approach works because the message is clear, the tone is all
positive, and the coach relates the salesperson's performance to her
business plan goals. Here's another example:

Dorothy—
I looked at last night's performance report. I saw you closed a deal
yesterday. You ought to be able to close at least five this month.

In this example, the coach communicates poorly because it is
unclear whether the tone is positive or not, and the coach makes
no reference to Dorothy's goals. This e-mail could mean either that
the coach is impressed with Dorothy's performance or disappointed in it. Regardless of what the coach expects to communicate, Dorothy may read the message and think the other way.

Ideally, communication between coach and salesperson occurs
face-to-face. Since this is not always possible, the second best is
voice-to-voice. When this is not an option, e-mail and voice mail
should be used, but the majority of these exchanges should deliver
specific positive feedback that references the salesperson's goals.

"How's It Going?"

Art Baumann, a Division Vice President of Sales Operations at Automatic Data Processing (ADP) TotalSource, believes in the approach that uses questions when following up to deliver feedback,
"Treat your salespeople like prospects. Help them discover what

you want them to learn through strategic questions." Here Art compares salespeople to prospects, because all salespeople know we are better off when we can ask the right questions to help the prospect understand why he should buy. In this approach, the coach asks the right questions to help the salesperson understand a certain piece of feedback for himself. This is analogous to the pushing and pulling that we discussed earlier. A salesperson is typically more likely to be "bought-in" to feedback that is pulled from his own lips through questioning than feedback that is simply pushed on him by a coach. We've seen a great deal of this follow-up success through questioning.

Earlier, we mentioned the very basic follow-up question: "How's it going?" Deciding to use this question as a conversation starter in follow-up did not come to us after reading a study by Harvard or MIT. Rather, after watching thousands of coaches follow up with their people, we've found the "How's it going?" approach to be the most effective. A coach doesn't become super coach automatically when he decides to get out of his chair and start walking around the office asking random salespeople, "How's it going?," although that approach would be a strong start for many coaches. The way it works best is when coaches ask, "How's it going so far on your goal of _____?" Then the next two questions are also quite helpful: "What's working for you so far?" "What's not working for you?" This basic three-question open-ended approach will yield the coach plenty of helpful data. (See Figure 5.2.)

The coach starts out by asking, "How's it going?" and references a salesperson's particular goal or action step. Regardless of the answer, the coach can then ask, "What's working so far for you as you head toward your goal?" In answering this question, the

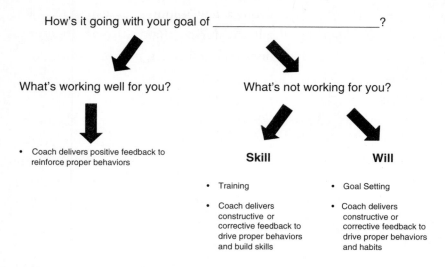

How's it going with your goal of _____?

What's working well for you?   What's not working for you?

- Coach delivers positive feedback to reinforce proper behaviors

Skill   **Will**

- Training
- Coach delivers constructive or corrective feedback to drive proper behaviors and build skills

- Goal Setting
- Coach delivers constructive or corrective feedback to drive proper behaviors and habits

FIGURE 5.2   How's It Going?

salesperson should highlight some successful outcomes or at least some behaviors that have been successful so far. Here is where the coach gives positive reinforcement to keep the salesperson doing the right things. This is a good way to make sure the feedback starts off on the right foot with positive recognition.

At this point the coach can ask, "What's not working so well for you?," which is another way of determining what the salesperson perceives to be the challenges he is facing as he tries to reach his goals. The salesperson may report a variety of issues here and the coach may have to ask deeper questions to learn more about what is really happening. Eventually, any challenges should boil down to either a skill issue, a will issue, or both. If a skill issue exists, the coach can either conduct an impromptu training session on the spot or schedule another time to conduct training. Regardless of whether the coach decides to conduct training immediately or later, the coach should devote a few minutes to delivering constructive or corrective feedback during this exchange (examples will follow.) If the coach discovers will issues, he can address these using a couple of different methods. First, the coach may want to have a quick goal-setting discussion with the salesperson. The coach can push or pull here, but the result of the conversation should be the salesperson becoming more focused on how his behavior right now is important to the ultimate realization of his goals and business plan. During this session in which the coach helps refocus the salesperson, the coach will likely deliver some constructive and/or corrective feedback with respect to the will and motivation of the salesperson.

As you can see from the explanation above, and will see from the examples to follow, the coach applies positive, constructive, and corrective feedback when following up, just as he did in the training context.

(AHS) My mother has been a star lobbyist in Annapolis, Maryland, for many years. Of course I like to brag, but she has been named one of "The Top 100 Professional Women in Maryland" numerous times over the years. During her career as a lobbyist, she has coached and mentored several less experienced people as they have entered the profession. One mentee in particular was a woman who had a great deal of talent and potential but also one slight challenge. She would often dress in black leather outfits with silver zippers all over them. My mother told us that her new mentee dressed like a dominatrix. It did not seem to be too significant an issue until one day my mother observed her mentee, dressed in full leather, addressing two very influential politicians. As she spoke with them, she slowly slid her pen in and out of her mouth. My mother could not let this go on much longer. When she had a chance to speak to the woman privately, she complimented her initiative in addressing the two politicians, and then explained how her attire and pen antics were unprofessional and could negatively impact her credibility. The mentee took some time, but eventually received the corrective feedback well and has gone on to become a successful lobbyist. Most coaches will probably never need to confront situations like this, but this example is another testament to the importance of coaches getting out of their offices and observing their people performing their jobs.

The following examples of follow-up/"How's it going?" conversations between coach and salesperson illustrate how this approach can be used to help salespeople achieve their goals.

Example 1

> *Coach:* Hey, Ben. I know you set your goal and planned in your schedule to complete your telephone prospecting on Wednesday mornings with your goals of 25 dials, 10 contacts, and 2 appointments. How's it going?
>
> *Salesperson:* I am experiencing total domination! It's only 9:30 and I'm already 20 dials, 10 contacts, and 3 appointments in. (Ben stands up to deliver a celebratory chest bump to his coach. This move is not a recommended best practice for all sales teams. Consult your HR staff before executing.)
>
> *Coach:* That's terrific, Ben. What's working so well for you?
>
> *Salesperson:* Well, for one, I'm really organized with my call list because I came in at 7 A.M. to create it, so I could start calling at 8 A.M. with no distractions in between calls.

Coach: I love your commitment. Doing that each Wednesday will have you up to 100 percent of your yearly goal in no time. It'll also get you on that new Harley you're always talking about.

Salesperson: That's what I'm saying.

Coach: Are you coming across any challenges? Anything not working well for you?

Salesperson: Just that you're here distracting me right now. I'm just teasing. No, no challenges. I'm *en fuego.*

Coach: It *is* getting kinda hot in here. I tell you what, you set another appointment by noon, and lunch at Chick-fil-A is on me.

Salesperson: You're on!

In this example, the coach followed the questioning template and learned that Ben was experiencing a great deal of success. Then the coach effectively delivered positive feedback to promote more of the right activity, and he connected the right activity to the fulfillment of the salesperson's professional and personal goals. Lastly, since Ben had already hit a portion of his goal with the appointments, the coach raised the goal to keep Ben motivated, and he offered an extra challenge. This is a great tactic and another reason to make sure coaches are spending time with their top performers, not just their newer or weaker people. Raising the bar keeps top performers from experiencing complacency.

"Unless a man undertakes more than he can possibly do, he will never do all that he can."

—Henry Drummond, Scottish theologian and scientist

Example 2

> *Coach:* Hey, Ben. I know you set your goal and planned in your schedule to complete your telephone prospecting on Wednesday mornings with your goal of 25 dials, 10 contacts, and 2 appointments. It's 10:30, how's it going?
>
> *Salesperson:* All right, I guess. Thirty dials, but only two contacts and one appointment.
>
> *Coach:* Thirty dials! You've already exceeded your goal of 25. What's working for you?
>
> *Salesperson:* I guess I've been real disciplined with my pace. I shut my door and tried to limit distractions, then just dialed away. Check out the callous on my dialing finger.
>
> *Coach:* Impressive. You may want to get that looked at. Your discipline is great, though. I know that's not easy. What's not working for you? Any challenges?
>
> *Salesperson:* These gatekeepers just own me today. I can't get by. I think they all attended some gatekeeper boot camp or something to learn how to screen me out.
>
> *Coach:* I feel your pain. What is your opening line?
>
> *Salesperson:* I think I just say, "Hello, this is Ben with The Next Level. May I speak to Mr. Big please?"
>
> *Coach:* Next time try to alter it slightly: "Good morning, this is Ben with The Next Level for Mr. Big please." It's very similar, but instead of asking for permission, you are expecting to be passed through.
>
> *Salesperson:* Interesting concept. I'll try that.
>
> *Coach:* Let me know how it goes. A few others have mentioned trouble with gatekeepers, so we will practice dealing with them at our sales meeting Monday. Keep up the good

work. With your fierce pace and your new opening line, I
bet you'll set a couple more appointments this morning.

In Example 2, the coach again followed the questioning template. He did a nice job of starting with the positive and compli-
menting Ben's pace and work ethic. Then the coach used
questioning to identify a skill issue—Ben was having trouble getting past the gatekeeper. The coach gave a quick training pointer
with some constructive feedback, then assured Ben that they would
address the skill gap in greater detail at the sales meeting. Finally,
the coach ended with encouragement and more positive feedback
to leave Ben feeling motivated.

Example 3

> *Coach:* Hey, Ben. I know you set your goal and planned in
> your schedule to complete your telephone prospecting on
> Wednesday mornings with your goal of 25 dials, 10 con-
> tacts, and 2 appointments. It's 10:30, how's it going?
>
> *Salesperson:* I'm on my way. Already three dials in.
>
> *Coach:* Okay. What's working well for you? Tell me about the
> three dials.
>
> Salesperson: No contacts yet, but I've got a really great list of
> prospects to call, so I'm looking forward to big results.
>
> *Coach:* Good. The list is important. It's already 10:30 though,
> and you set the goal in our last GSM to spend all morning
> Wednesday on the phone. What's getting in your way?
>
> *Salesperson:* I'm cool, coach. I didn't get in until 10 today be-
> cause I had a tanning appointment, and they couldn't see
> me until 9. Don't I look fine?

Coach: Yes, but I'm a bit confused. Help me understand why you scheduled a tanning appointment during the telephone prospecting time that you committed to in our last GSM, so that you would make sure you hit your goals for the month and stay on track for your business plan.

Salesperson: Gee, I guess I didn't look at it like that. If I don't hit my goals then I won't be able to afford that big vacation anyway, in which case my tan won't even matter.

Coach: You said it.

Salesperson: How about this? I don't have any appointments this afternoon, so I'll keep dialing into the afternoon until I hit my goals. And I guess I can move my tanning appointments to the evening.

Coach: Now we're talking. I tell you what, you hit your two appointments today, and your next tanning session is on me.

The coach followed the questioning model in this example too. There was not too much for Ben to brag about, but he did point out his solid list. Then after asking about the challenges, the coach uncovered a significant will issue. The coach responded well by referencing Ben's recent GSM goal and business plan. Then the coach was able to pull corrective feedback from Ben to get him back on track. Despite the poor effort from Ben, the coach still ended in a manner that motivated him to perform.

In each of these examples, the coach identifies the skill or will issues fairly easily. That's not always the case. Often it takes asking several more questions or, in the scenarios above, the coach may have to sit down and listen to a few calls. This act of doing the job with the salesperson is "coaching in the crunch" and that will be the focus in Chapter 6.

Summary

Let's sum up this section on follow-up, as we continue to strive to create a great salesperson. First of all, regular and consistent follow-up is the best way to ensure that salespeople are working toward their business plans and the goals set during GSMs. The best coaches follow-up all the time, and the best salespeople appreciate the extra accountability. Coaches execute this follow-up by simply walking around (or calling or e-mailing) while people are doing the job and asking, "How's it going?" Then they create a discussion by asking, "What's working?" and "What's not working?" This dialogue enables coaches and salespeople to uncover skill and will issues, which sets up more opportunities for training, goal setting, and feedback—positive, constructive, and corrective.

Now get ready to spend even more time with your coach if you're a salesperson, or with your salespeople if you're a coach. We've trained; we've followed up; now it's time to coach in the crunch!

6

Coaching in the Crunch

(AHS) I have a friend named Bobby who has spent a large portion of his successful career in sales and sales management positions. One of the things that makes Bobby so successful as a coach and salesperson is his enthusiasm and endless optimism. Early in his career as a salesperson, Bobby had a day in which his sales coach was riding along in the car with him to visit some of his key customers. The day was going well until one particular sales call, when at the beginning of the meeting the decision maker at an important account expressed some disappointment: "I like working with you Bobby, but it seems lately that you've really been dancing around some of these service issues." Without hesitation, Bobby dove from his chair onto the floor and executed several iterations of the worm right in the customer's office. Bobby stood up and proclaimed: "Now that's dancing around your service issues!" After overcoming the initial shock, all three people in the room laughed at Bobby's attempt to make light of the situation. Subsequently, Bobby went on to address each of the customer's concerns and built an even stronger relationship with the account. The two lessons here are, first, as a salesperson it can be a good idea to use humor to address a challenging situation; and second, as a coach, it's a good idea to get out of the office, coach in the crunch, and watch your salespeople do the job, because they will do almost anything to impress you.

Returning to the coaching model, we will review where we are in the process of creating a great salesperson. Coach and salesperson have created and agreed upon a business plan. The pair has conducted regularly scheduled goal-setting meetings to stay on track. Along the way they have identified skill and will issues, which are addressed through training and continued goal-setting respectively. All along, throughout hours, days, weeks, and months, the coach is following up and asking, "how's it going?" to continuously make sure that the salesperson's efforts are in line with his plans. We are nearing the completion of our creation of greatness but are not quite there yet. The next step is to make sure that coach and salesperson spend time in the crunch, that is, doing the salesperson's job together. See Figure 6.1.

Coaching in the crunch is when coach and salesperson are in those moments of truth, executing the salesperson's plan together, and working in a meeting or over the phone with a live prospect or client. They prepare together, execute together, and debrief together after the session. For the purposes of this section, when we refer to a "sales call" it can be a face-to-face or telephone interaction.

FIGURE 6.1   Coaching Model 6

"When coaches are in the field with people, they gain respect and credibility as leaders and people are more willing to learn from them. Managers need credibility on the streets. They need to prove to their people that they 'get it.' "

—Joe Mastalia, President and
sales leader at DePasquale
Salon Systems

Mastalia leads several sales teams at DePasquale, where he has driven very aggressive sales growth. One of DePasquale's keys to success is that each sales coach is required to spend at least two full days each week out in the field coaching in the crunch.

"Sales managers can't stop selling. You need to show your people you can still make it happen. Continuing to go out and sell enables you to stay relevant with your team. Get out of your office and stop managing spreadsheets."

—Kevin Kelley, Assistant
Vice President of Fleet
Services, a division of
Enterprise Rent-A-Car

There are very few activities that should be higher on a sales coach's priority list than coaching in the crunch. In every sales organization we work with, the top performing teams are led by coaches who spend more time in the crunch than all the other coaches do. Also, coaching in the crunch is the coach's best opportunity to earn street cred. The best coaches create a dynamic in which their salespeople aspire to be like them. When salespeople see their coach's ability to interact with customers and perform at a higher level than they can, they look up to their coach and value the relationship even more.

When coaching in the crunch, the coach can play three primary roles: the leader, the supporter, or the observer. Next we will discuss each scenario.

The Leader

The coach assumes the role of leader when he is the one conducting the greater part of the sales call. This approach is particularly beneficial for brand new salespeople, for times when the coach and salesperson have recently started working together, or when a salesperson needs to understand exactly what the coach expects. This experience is very helpful in transitioning a salesperson from unconscious and incompetent behaviors to conscious and incompetent ones—the salesperson moves from not knowing what he doesn't know to knowing what he doesn't know. Prior to the actual call, the duo prepares together, with the coach demonstrating what to do during pre-call planning. In addition to demonstrating the proper preparation habits, the coach must be prepared to deliver a cash-money demonstration. The coach will also review her strategy and objectives for the call with the salesperson before and after the call.

During the actual call, the salesperson primarily observes and takes notes while the coach leads the meeting. It is the coach's job to model all the right behaviors. Following the call, the pair debriefs to recount what worked and what did not work. It's also important to review what the salesperson learned from the experience. The main objective of this approach is for the salesperson to receive a strong demonstration of how to conduct a sales call and, as a result, be able to ramp up more quickly.

There are a few challenges to be aware of. Some coaches enjoy selling and still need the adrenaline rush and recognition they received when they were salespeople. If that is the case, they will play the role of the leader but never relinquish all the control. This can halt the team's ability to grow to its potential because the coach can never effectively sell everything for the entire team. One solution to this challenge is for the coach not always to play the role of leader, just to get a sale. The coach must realize that after being the leader once or twice she must conduct more training and give the salesperson more opportunities to practice.

Another potential challenge in using the leader approach is that the salesperson can become overly dependent on the coach and expect all sales calls to occur like this one. This is obviously unrealistic. The way to avoid this problem is to make sure the coach sets proper expectations as to how coaching in the crunch works—first leader, then supporter, and finally observer. This way the salesperson knows that he will eventually need to step up and make it happen on his own.

One of the hazards of using the leader method is that the customer may want to continue a relationship exclusively with the coach. The coach cannot be the contact for all of the team's customers. This challenge is typically best addressed by having the coach set expectations with the customer at the start of the call. Depending on the scenario, the coach may say something like, "I will be leading today's meeting. Moving forward, however, we will be supporting you as an organization, so Howie, your account executive, will be your primary point of contact."

The Supporter

The coach assumes the role of supporter in scenarios when the salesperson is leading the greater part of the call. The coach is there to keep the salesperson on track and give help as needed. Utilizing this scenario is most beneficial for a salesperson that may be at the conscious and competent stage, but may still need to build some confidence. The supporter approach sets up a good opportunity for the coach to catch her salespeople doing things very well. Before embarking on one of these calls, the coach and salesperson need to conduct lots of training and practice sessions, and work through as many potential scenarios as possible so that the salesperson feels ready to take on the world. If there is driving required, the salesperson and coach should try to ride together, and the coach should drive. That way the coach can play the role of the prospect or client and the salesperson can practice his role. It is important too that the duo discusses any specific areas in which they believe the coach may need to step in to provide extra muscle.

During a supporter call, the salesperson does as much as he can, only bringing the coach in if necessary. In this scenario, the coach should be taking careful notes so that after the call she can deliver specific feedback. During the debriefing (perhaps in the car) the pair can discuss what worked and what did not work and think about what the salesperson might do differently next time.

The supporter approach is a great opportunity for a salesperson to be a star in front of the coach, in a real situation with a prospect or client. Remember Bobby and the worm? Also, many clients appreciate this approach because they feel they are receiving special attention since the coach is attending the meeting.

It is important that the coach remembers that it is acceptable for the salesperson to make mistakes. Unless the mistake is earth-shattering, the coach should not intervene in the call. Remember that making mistakes is the best way to learn. If the coach takes over too much in the call and corrects the salesperson, she can potentially destroy the salesperson's confidence. This may make the salesperson resistant to future coaching in the crunch opportunities and slow his development. The other challenge with this approach happens when there is not enough training and practice prior to the call. The salesperson takes the meeting way off track and blows the deal. If this happens, the coach is often just as guilty as the salesperson, if not more so. Prior to a supporter call, it is the coach's job to get the salesperson ready. It is also the coach's job to determine when they are ready to transfer from a leader call to a supporter call. Next is an example of a particularly memorable supporter call.

(AHS) It was a pretty big opportunity for me—my first major sales presentation at The Next Level, in which I would really be taking the lead. My sales coach, Steve, was there with me, primarily in the supporter role, so I wanted to impress him too. I was presenting to a company with a sales force of several thousand people that had a very positive reputation and had the potential to become a great client and partner. I had practiced my presentation numerous times on Steve the night before until he fell asleep. Then I reviewed it on the mirror until I felt confident, bulletproof, and handsome.

In the morning, after a workout and a healthy breakfast, I was ready to go. We walked from our hotel over to the prospective client's office and were greeted in the lobby by Wendy, vice president of sales operations, a sharp, confident, and well-respected woman in her organization. She explained to us that, unfortunately,

Jim, the vice president of sales, whom we had also planned to present to, would not be at the meeting because he had a health emergency with one of his dogs. She assured us that we would be fine because she would include her teammate Ashley in the meeting, and the two of them were the decision makers. We had flown from Los Angeles to Atlanta for this meeting, so I was determined to give it everything I had.

Wendy and I went back and forth like Rock-em Sock-em robots during the presentation, with me trying to answer each of her challenging questions with a positive solution to her sales team's situation. All in all, the presentation went well, but when I asked for the order, I was unable to get the yes. Wendy and Ashley wanted to take some more time to discuss their options.

Steve and I left the meeting, feeling decent about our chances to win the deal. As we were walking through the parking lot, we heard a car honk its horn and heard: "Steve and Adam, is that you?" It was Jim, VP of sales. He got out of his car, greeted us, and apologized for missing our meeting. As he was speaking to Steve and me and explaining the life-threatening situation with his dog, I noticed his eyes peering down to my midsection. Jim then pointed toward the zipper on my pants, so I naturally looked down, only to see that my fly was unzipped. I had just stood up and delivered a two-hour sales presentation to two women with my fly open. After I got over some minor embarrassment and the three of us shared a few laughs, I felt better about the whole incident: "Maybe the reason Wendy and Ashley did not buy is because they were distracted by my fly and were unable to focus on all my key points?"

Steve and I scheduled a time to follow up with Jim and were then off to the airport to head to our next engagement. We continued to laugh about my mishap in the cab until the Nigerian cab

driver became interested and asked what had happened. So Steve told the entire story to the driver. After sharing a laugh with us he asked: "I only have one question . . . did it jump out?"

Thankfully, the answer is no, it did not jump out, but Steve and I did share several more laughs reliving our cab driver's interesting question. Since that day, the prospect has become a great client, and Steve and I have continued to jump out—not jump out of our pants, but jump out within our sales, sales coaching, and consulting careers. We hope that you are ready to do the same.

The supporter coaching role, which Steve played above, is a great transitional step between the leader and the next scenario, the observer role.

The Observer

"If man can make penicillin out of moldy bread, just think about what you can do with yourself."
—Zig Ziglar, author and speaker

When a coach can confidently become the observer, it is clear that the salesperson has truly transitioned from moldy bread to penicillin. This approach is typically used with the highly competent salespeople on the team. In fact, many coaches believe that when they can truly be an observer on a call (which is not easy, because most coaches have trouble keeping their mouths shut), they have reached the pinnacle as a coach, at least with that particular salesperson. In this role, the coach simply observes and listens during the call. When a coach has reached this level, it means that all the repetitious skill training and practice sessions have worked!

Before one of these calls, a lot of the same steps need to happen. The salesperson can lead the preparation, but the pair still needs to practice and discuss the strategy and specific tactics. Here the coach can pull the plan from the salesperson and should not have to push many ideas on the situation—the salesperson knows how to prepare. During the actual meeting the coach's job is simple, but not easy—sit there, take notes, and don't intervene unless it is absolutely necessary. Then after the call, the duo will hopefully be celebrating a great client or prospect interaction. After this type of call, there may be some small tweaking and specific feedback to discuss, but it should just be very fine tuning.

The only major challenge to this approach is that the coach must not participate. We repeat this message because it's hard for the coach not to engage. The entire point of this type of call, however, is to let the salesperson use his own techniques and style. The primary reason that the two of you are able to conduct an "observer" type call is because you have determined before the call that the salesperson is able to lead a call without any involvement from the coach. So that is how the call must be executed. If the coach commits to not becoming involved and fails on her commitment, she may be seriously damaging the relationship with the salesperson or diminishing the salesperson's confidence.

There are tremendous benefits to using this approach when it is executed properly. First of all, when this strong-performing salesperson shines in front of the coach by executing a great call, the coach will develop even more confidence in that team member. This is also a wonderful opportunity for the coach to deliver some powerful positive feedback when she observes the salesperson executing so many of the right behaviors on the call. After receiving the praise and recognition, the salesperson will be more receptive to hearing constructive feedback (if there is any) regarding the finer points of the call because he will be feeling so confident. Finally, this is a great way for the coach to observe the top performing salespeople's best practices, which will enable the coach to tell stories that motivate others and use those best practices in training sessions with other team members.

(AHS) I have worked with a strong, confident, independent salesperson named Melissa at General Electric. For many years at GE, Melissa has been a top sales performer in each of the several divisions in which she has worked. Because Melissa is a top performer, when her coaches have "coached in the crunch" with her, they have typically taken the "observer" approach. Melissa makes sales presentations to groups of GE customers and her coaches often sit in the room to observe. Melissa described the experiences she had with two of her recent coaches as being extremely different from each other. One of her coaches would sit in the room to observe her presentations and would often leave the room to take or make calls on his cell phone. After Melissa's presentation, this coach would shower her with praise and give her general feedback about her strong presentation and thank her for her great sales results. Melissa appreciated the recognition but never really connected to this coach because she always felt the feedback was not genuine. Her other coach utilizes a different approach when observing Melissa's presentations. He turns off his cell phone and takes copious notes throughout the entire meeting. After Melissa's presentation, this coach takes Melissa out for a cup of coffee and, over the next half hour, highlights specific things Melissa said or did well, and specific areas where he would make adjustments. Melissa values these sessions because she knows that this coach has her best

interests in mind and delivers genuine useful feedback, both positive and constructive. Although he is no longer her supervisor,
Melissa still looks to this former coach as an informal mentor.

The lesson here is that top performers love attention from their
coaches. There is a myth in many sales organizations that sales
coaches should just leave top performers alone and let them do their
thing. Coaches should be careful, because often "their thing" could
become staying put and performing only until another sales coach
from a competitor or headhunter contacts them and shows them
greener pastures. Obviously a coach's approach and time spent with a
top performer will differ from the way he works with a green bean
or mediocre performer, but everyone needs love and attention. Often top performing salespeople can be the most open to sincere constructive feedback because they know how hard it is to perform, and
since they probably already have a solid sales process, they can easily
incorporate new ideas to their existing approach.

Assume that a certain sales coach has the ability to improve a
salesperson's performance by X percent with each day that coach
spends with a salesperson. (If you have made it this far in the book,
your X should be a positive number (i.e., you are making a positive
impact on results). If your X is negative and you are a sales coach,
the best way for you to help your organization is to not come to
work.) Should the sales coach be spending that day with a top producer to improve his performance by X percent or with a weak
producer to improve his performance by X percent? The stronger
the producer, the stronger the positive impact that the effective
sales coach can have on performance. Obviously, to run an effective
team, a coach needs to spend time with all of her people. The best
coaches we have seen, however, spend the majority of their time

coaching rookies, working with top performers to clear obstacles, and delivering praise and feedback.

(AHS) When I was a rookie at The Next Level, my sales manager, Steve, and I had the chance to go on a great call together. To this point our company had done a significant amount of work in the financial services industry, but there was one particular firm we had not yet broken into. After much persistence, Steve finally secured an initial appointment with the key decision maker over the sales force at this great prospect. Since I was so new, the plan was for Steve to play the leader role in this call. I was pretty excited because it was one of the first major sales calls I was able to be a part of at The Next Level. I was looking forward to seeing Steve in action since he had always been considered a real "rainmaker." I knew he would be doing most of the work on the call and that it was my job to just take notes and listen. We walked into the large Manhattan skyscraper lobby and checked in with security. After about ten minutes of waiting at the security desk, we were asked to head up to the 32nd floor for our meeting. I knew Steve was very excited about the opportunity ahead of us because he had been talking about it since he had set the appointment weeks ago. So we walk into the elevator, and it is just Steve and I in the nicely decorated mirrored elevator, on our way up to the meeting. A couple of floors into our ride I see Steve look into the mirror, which I assume is to check his appearance. Then he startles me by belting out, "I feel good! I feel great! I've got a sale to make and I can't wait!" I start to become a bit concerned for both of us. Here we are headed into this big sales call, and Steve has turned into a loon. More than that, I started thinking, 'what have I signed up for?' Here was this guy who was supposed to be my new manager, who was supposed to be my teacher and mentor in this new business, and he was a complete whacko. So I turn to Steve to ask him what's going on, and he just looks right back into the mirror and exclaims: "I'm terrific, I'm tremendous, and when I close, I'm stupendous!" He gave me more of the same nonsense.

Fortunately, by the time we had arrived at our meeting Steve had returned to normal. He conducted the meeting with a great deal of positive enthusiasm and moved the sale forward. The call actually ended a bit early because, after about 45 minutes, the lights went out. This just happened to be the day of the blackout in New York City. Since that meeting we have done a fair amount of work with the client, but what has really stuck with me was Steve's elevator show prior to the call. I realized after seeing Steve in the meeting that he was simply using positive self-talk to get him in the right frame of mind immediately before the call. While I thought it was a bit hokey at the time and was not a huge believer at first, I will admit that, through practice of my own, I have become a strong advocate of positive self-talk. I do it all the time now, and I believe it helps me succeed. Just this morning, before I stepped into the shower, I looked at myself in the mirror and said, "I feel good! I feel great! I've got a book to write and I can't wait!"

The point here is that in order for a coach to coach in the crunch effectively while playing the role of "the leader," he must deliver a great demonstration of all parts of the sales process, before, during, and after the call.

We have painted a rosy picture of all the great reasons to coach in the crunch. After all, most salespeople love it. They are getting the attention and recognition that salespeople appreciate. Additionally, through helpful and specific feedback, salespeople are able to really improve their skills after spending time in the crunch with their coach. Lastly, since the coach is often an experienced salesperson, salespeople like having their coach interacting with customers because it can help improve the relationship with the account.

It's also important to be aware of why some salespeople will resist coaching in the crunch opportunities. Some will say they do not like being put on the spot. This is often code for, "I'm not as confident as I need to be yet." So, if a salesperson lacks that confidence, it may be best to start with the leader approach to coaching in the crunch, so the salesperson does not feel like he is on the spot right away. Others may resist because they may be mediocre performers and not want to have their coach see the poor relationships they have with customers. This can be another opportunity for training to address skill or will issues, and again it would probably make sense to start with the leader approach to coaching in the crunch. Lastly, some salespeople may be reluctant to spend time in the crunch with their coach because they may find it difficult to receive feedback. If this is the case, the coach must go out of her way to catch the salesperson doing things right. Beginning exchanges with positive feedback often makes the salesperson more receptive to the more constructive feedback. This challenge can also be overcome during pre-call practice sessions. If the coach gives flawless demonstrations, the salespeople will start to become more open to feedback when they realize they are teamed up with a seasoned master.

Here are a few more coaching in the crunch best practices to consider whether you are a coach or a salesperson.

- The salesperson should confirm the scheduled meeting(s) so that the duo does not spend time practicing for a call that never happens.

- Ideally, the pair can spend the entire day together so they can meet in the morning to strategize the day; coach in the crunch across several calls, with feedback sessions in between calls; and debrief at the end of the day.
- Some coaches like to implement surprise coaching in the crunch visits during which they just happen to be in the neighborhood and show up at a call. If a strong trust is established between both parties, the salesperson should be excited about these occasions.
- When coaching in the crunch, it is best to ride in the same car so you can prepare and debrief before and after.

When salesperson and coach are together coaching in the crunch, one way to accelerate the skill building is with a call certification or evaluation process. Refer to the coaching in the crunch tool shown in Figure 6.2. This one is used by our clients at De-Pasquale, where sales coaches coach in the crunch with salon consultants who sell beauty products to salons. For more coaching in the crunch certification tools, visit www.nextlevelsalesconsulting.com.

> *"Having a call coaching format is critical because it makes riding along more formal and consistent. Usually the manager and salesperson just leave the call and give a big high five. Now there is more structure so the feedback is more specific and salespeople know what to repeat and what to avoid next time."*
>
> —Debbie Hood, sales executive,
> Countrywide

The teammates are not just riding along to ride along, but they have a context now to deliver specific and immediate coaching,

DePasquale Car Coaching (Coaching in th Crunch)

Salon Consultant: _____

Coach: _____

Date: _____

1 = Below Expectations
3 = Meets Expectations
5 = Exceeds Expectations

Item	Y N	Quality					Accounts				
Pre-Call Planning		1	2	3	4	5					
Presentation Book		1	2	3	4	5					
Write Order with the Account		1	2	3	4	5					
Daily Sales Activity Report		1	2	3	4	5					
Inventory Control Use		1	2	3	4	5					
Promotional Discussion		1	2	3	4	5					
Talk To Decision Maker		1	2	3	4	5					
Routing/Time Management		1	2	3	4	5					
Overall Sales Skills		1	2	3	4	5					
Green Book/Profile Book		1	2	3	4	5					

Comments:
_____
_____
_____

Strengths:
_____
_____
_____

Improvement areas:
_____
_____
_____

Action steps:
_____
_____
_____

FIGURE 6.2   Coaching in the Crunch

and they can document progress over several coaching in the crunch experiences. You and your team can use these tools after each shared call or after a day spent coaching in the crunch.

Many strong sales organizations set certain scores or benchmarks that salespeople can shoot for when they are in the crunch with their coach. When the salespeople hit certain scores, they become certified at a specific level and often receive some sort of basic recognition, like a plaque or certificate, from the company.

Having a scoring system and related incentive program is another way to generate enthusiasm toward coaching in the crunch from both salespeople and coaches. Salespeople will look forward to time with their coach because they know they will be scored and will have the chance to become certified. Coaches will resist the urge to always be the leader on calls together, because they will want to have the opportunity to evaluate their salespeople and move them through the certification process.

"Coaching is rolling up your sleeves and showing people how to do things."

—Tom Chelew, Vice President
of Fleet Services, a division
of Enterprise Rent-A-Car

On great sales teams, coaching in the crunch is one of the most enjoyable parts of the job for both salesperson and coach. Sales can be a lonely job for a salesperson; when they are in the crunch, they get a partner to execute and have fun with. For the coach, this is what it is all about. You probably became a coach because you wanted to build great salespeople. In the crunch is where this happens best!

7 | Sales Meetings and Huddles

"The strength of the wolf is the pack. The strength of the pack is the wolf."

—Rudyard Kipling,
writer and poet

(AHS) We recently held a focus group with one of our client's team of sales coaches. There were about 15 coaches in the room along with the president of their company, Steve, and me. We were facilitating a dialogue with the team to learn more about the strengths and challenges that the teams were currently facing with respect to running meaningful and motivating meetings. One of the company's top managers, Craig LoGrande, raised his hand and admitted, "Every month I run one sales meeting, and attend another sales meeting for our sales managers, and I've gotta tell you . . . I've never walked out of my meeting or someone else's meeting feeling motivated."

To make this comment in front of the group took some chutz-pah, but his comment is an accurate description of most meetings. In fact, many times we have observed that sales meetings are more like sales beatings, so people leave them dejected rather than in-spired. Other times, salespeople feel like meetings are a waste of the time that they could be using to sell more to earn a living. As Mike Mejia, Vice President of Sales at Adelphia says, "If a meeting is just to have a meeting—it's de-motivating."

In this chapter, the goal is to put a plan in place that will enable you and your sales team to conduct sales meetings that are positive, motivating, and useful. Imagine that—a sales meeting that every-one (coach and salespeople) can look forward to attending.

The Coaching Model

You may be getting a bit tired of this coaching model by now (see Figure 7.1), but the truth is, each segment of the model represents another opportunity for the coach to communicate with salespeo-ple in a way that inspires stronger performance, which leads to the ultimate goal of success for everyone on the team.

Most of what has been covered so far has addressed skills and techniques specific to the coach-salesperson one-on-one dy-namic. The coach and salesperson agree on a business plan to-gether, they conduct one-on-one GSMs regularly, they conduct individualized training to address specific skills, the coach follows up to reinforce each salesperson's individual priorities, and the

FIGURE 7.1   Coaching Model 7

coach and salesperson do the job together one-on-one during coaching in the crunch. A sales meeting is obviously a huge opportunity for the entire team because the dynamic changes to one in which everyone is together. The coach and salespeople can deliver one consistent message to everyone on the team at the same time. What a great way to sculpt great salespeople!

Professor and author Peter Drucker, in his *Harvard Business Review* article from June 2004, *What Makes an Effective Executive*, outlines the eight practices that are common to effective executives. One of the practices is that they run effective meetings. This is critical because, as Drucker states in the article, "even junior executives and professionals are with other people—that is, in a meeting of some sort—more than half of every business day." This is why it is necessary to make that time productive. As Drucker states, "Making a meeting productive takes a good deal of self-discipline. It requires that executives determine what kind of meeting is appropriate and stick to that format. It's also necessary to terminate the meeting as soon as its specific purpose has been accomplished." The good news for us is that, for the purposes of this book, we are concerned with only one type of meeting—the sales meeting. Therefore we can share with you a format that has been successful for top sales coaches and their teams, and then stick to it.

The challenge is that many of us have preconceived barriers that have been built up over time from years of attending ineffective meetings. Before looking at some of the reasons why salespeople can have a negative attitude toward meetings, let's try to start with a clean slate—a positive attitude.

A great friend and colleague of ours, Mark Norman, recently told us of a rural community in Iowa that is so small it seems to have only one of everything important—one grocery store, one movie theater, one high school, and one barber shop. Usually that's part of the appeal of smaller towns; everyone gets to know everyone else. The problem in this community happens to be with the barber shop. It is the only shop in town, and the owner is the only barber within a 100-mile radius. When the men in town need to get their hair cut they must visit this particular barber. This would not be an issue if this barber weren't one of the most negative individuals you could ever come across. He's the ultimate pessimist, so much of a downer that he actually earned a nickname in the community: "The Negative Barber."

One afternoon, a man named Chad walked into the Negative Barber's shop for a haircut. The exact opposite of the barber, Chad was always smiling, he had a skip in his step, and it was obvious that he was excited to be alive. Those of you who know some negative people know that positive people can rub negative people the wrong way. After Chad sat down in the Negative Barber's chair, their conversation went like this:

Negative Barber: The weather has been terrible, the economy stinks, there's war in many parts of the world. What on earth are you so excited about?

Chad: You know, I'm glad you asked! My wife and I have been saving for the last ten years for a trip to Italy. And we are finally going! We're leaving tomorrow. That's why I'm getting my hair cut.

Negative Barber: Italy? My wife and I went to Italy a few years back. The people were rude, the cities were dirty, and the weather was horrible the whole time we were there. Maybe you should go somewhere else?

Chad: The trip is already booked.

Negative Barber: That's too bad. How are you getting over to Europe?

Chad: We're flying on Premier Airlines. We got a pretty good deal!

Negative Barber: Premier, huh? My wife and I flew Premier. The flight attendants were nasty, the bathroom doors on the plane were locked the entire way over to Europe, and they lost our luggage. I wouldn't get too excited. Hey, where are you staying over there?

Chad: The Rome Paradise Inn. We've heard good things.

Negative Barber: Good things? This is really ironic. My wife and I must have used the same travel agent. We stayed there too. The pillows were hard, the wake-up calls came late, and the food at the hotel restaurant was disgusting. Is it too late to change?

Chad: I think so. It's a package deal.

Negative Barber: Why you going to Italy anyway? I'd just cancel the whole trip if I were you.

Chad: My wife and I are devout Catholics. We've been waiting our whole lives for a personal visit with the Pope.

Negative Barber: Ha! Did you just say personal visit with the Pope? Let me tell you what's going to happen. You are going to walk into St. Peter's Square at the Vatican. You and about 10,000 other people will be expecting your "personal visit." The pope will be about a half mile away and if you're lucky, you'll see the back of his head. Good luck.

Chad leaves the barber shop, not quite as enthusiastic as he was when he entered. He and his wife go to Italy and return 10 days later. About two months go by, and Chad just can't wait any longer. He must go see the Negative Barber to get a trim. So he walks in, and as the Negative Barber starts to trim Chad's hair he recognizes him:

Negative Barber: Hey! I remember you. You're the guy who went to Italy. Terrible, right?

Chad: Italy was delightful. The people were friendly, the cities were clean, and the weather was perfect every day.

Negative Barber: What about those flights? The worst, right?

Chad: You know what? The flight attendants were pleasant, the bathrooms were pristine with no lines, and our luggage was actually waiting for us when we stepped off the plane.

Negative Barber: All right—that Paradise Inn. They couldn't have made that place any better.

Chad: My wife and I loved it. The pillows were cottony soft, all our wake-up calls were on time, and the food at the restaurant was delicious. We ate most of our meals there.

Negative Barber: Fine. You went for the Pope. How was your personal visit?

Chad: You're not going to believe this. That was the best part. My wife and I got to St. Peter's Square, and the place was like a morgue. It must have been some sort of holiday in Rome, but no one else was around. So my wife and I walked up to the front of the square where the Pope usually stands at the altar. The altar door was cracked so I pushed it open and guess who was inside? The Pope, himself. When the Pope heard us enter, he slowly motioned both my wife and me to come toward him. Then he had us each kneel before him. He looked at us, placed his hand on my head, and you know what he said? "Where'd you get that lousy haircut?"

Clearly you can go about life looking for the positive, like Chad, or the not so positive, like the Negative Barber. After working with hundreds of thousands of salespeople, we have realized that individuals who show up for sales or training meetings typically fall into one of four categories. The 4-point system or "E-scale" categorizes each type of team member. E stands for enthusiasm, and the four levels characterize how enthusiastic someone is at the meeting:

- *4 on the E-scale is a Learner.* This person shows up early with extra sharpened pencils to take down every important note. Learners want to gain as much as possible from the meeting because they know they will be able to apply the information in the field. Learners typically participate very actively during the meeting.
- *3 on the E-scale is a Vacationer.* This person is out of his or her regular work environment for a little while so he or she treats it like a "vacation." Sometimes vacationers put their feet up and leave their sunglasses on during the meeting. These people tend to be semi-engaged in some parts of the meeting and enjoy seeing their friends and taking a short break from the job.
- *2 on the E-scale is a Hostage.* This person is at the meeting for one and only one reason—because she is required to be. Hostages do not typically disrupt the meeting; they just keep to themselves and participate only when they are absolutely forced to.
- *1 on the E-scale is a Terrorist.* This is a hostage with a bad attitude. Terrorists are negative and cynical and see it as their job to bring other meeting attendees down with them.

Where were you on the E-scale in the last meeting you attended?

We know everyone cannot be a 4 every day at every meeting. The key here is, whether you are a salesperson or a coach, you must be aware that all four types may be at your meeting. Once it is evident where each attendees is on the scale, try to spend time with and channel your energy toward the people that want to be there. Learners are ideal attendees—they want to get better and help others improve. You should work to harness their energy and transfer it to others. Vacationers and hostages are acceptable. See it as your challenge to try to use meeting activities and participation to get them up on the E-scale through the course of the meeting. Terrorists must be confronted and redirected. It is one thing to sabotage one's own career and motivation, but it is not acceptable to do so to others. Consistent terrorism can kill a positive sales culture.

While salespeople can go into meetings at varying levels on the E-scale, there are some common reasons why salespeople occasionally head into sales meetings with the Negative Barber type of outlook that exists at the lower end of the scale:

- Salespeople sometimes think the meeting will be all about the product(s) without much time devoted to how to sell the product.
- Salespeople perceive meetings as a waste of time if they don't think they will be learning anything new.
- Salespeople become frustrated when they have to take the time to attend meetings because that is time away from selling.
- Salespeople do not like meetings when the leader is not an effective facilitator, if his tone is not motivating and engaging.

- Salespeople become bored in meetings if there is no interaction and participation from the group. If the coach just uses the meeting to make announcements, salespeople become frustrated.
- Salespeople do not like it when meetings start or end late.
- Salespeople have low expectations when they attend meetings that do not have a written agenda. They know the discussion will not be focused and will end up on unproductive tangents.
- Salespeople are disappointed when sales meetings become operational meetings.
- Salespeople do not appreciate when the meeting leader uses a meeting to criticize poor performance and it becomes a beating versus a meeting.
- Some salespeople have a negative attitude toward meetings because they think they already know it all.
- Salespeople learn to hate meetings when they often become gripe sessions full of cynical complaints.
- Some salespeople who are not performing well are reluctant to go to sales meetings when they know their sales results will be reported.

Have any of these perceptions existed among your sales team?

What follows are all the reasons to have sales meetings despite the negative expectations that may exist among the team. Once your team is on track following the meeting model in this chapter, your sales meetings will be very well received, and people will be much less reluctant to attend. So why do you have the meetings?

- Meetings are a great venue to engage the team in team building or morale boosting exercises. Sales is a tough field, and it's easy to get down on oneself as a salesperson who is out there fighting the battles on one's own. The camaraderie that happens at sales meetings can be extremely inspiring.

- Meetings are one of the best venues to deliver recognition. Everyone loves being told they did a good job, especially when it is in front of peers. Public recognition at meetings motivates salespeople and impacts retention positively.

- Sales meetings are a great place to share success stories. When salespeople report their wins back to the team, others are motivated and able to incorporate each other's best practices. Sharing success stories helps keep the meeting tone positive and spirited.

- Sales meetings provide opportunities to focus or redirect the entire team toward specific goals. Maybe there is a push to move a certain product or capitalize on a special promotion. Sales meetings are a great way to get everyone on board.

- Great coaches and teams use sales meetings to ensure accountability. The coach and salespeople individually report their performances to the group and set goals in front of the group. This public peer reporting is an easy and effective way to hold team members accountable.

- Teams have had a lot of success using sales meetings as a forum to build relationships with other functions within the company. For example, many top sales teams invite service people or administrative people to the meetings. They typically love being included and everyone's job becomes easier because more people are on the same page.

- Good sales meetings often involve peer training and coaching from the more senior salespeople to the newer ones. This is a great way to develop future leaders within the team for the company and keeps seasoned veterans excited about the meetings.

- You can make the meetings fun. Some teams conduct training in the form of a game or give out special incentives at meetings to keep the team inspired.

How do you get all this done without having your meeting last all week? Follow the sample agenda in the next section. Obviously you'll need to adapt the agenda to your sales environment, but this should give you a pretty solid start.

The Sales Meeting

Here is an agenda for a well run, motivating, interactive, and useful meeting that takes less than one hour. Next we'll break down the steps and discuss how top coaches and salespeople execute each portion of the meeting.

■ Opening Inspiration	(2 minutes)
■ Success Stories	(1 minute/team member)
■ Training	(25 minutes)
■ Scoreboard—Goal Reporting and Setting	(10 minutes)
■ Summary and Action Items	(5 minutes)
■ Next Meeting Logistics and Assignment	(2 minutes)
■ Closing Inspiration	(1 minute)

Opening Inspiration

Anyone can brighten a room. Some people brighten it when they enter; others brighten the room when they leave. To start a sales meeting, a coach must do whatever it takes to get in the mood of someone who brightens the room upon entrance. Use positive self-talk, drink an energy drink, listen to your favorite song, or do 10 jumping jacks— whatever works for you. You may be about to encounter some negativity if you have some sad singers or slow walkers coming into the meeting for any of the reasons we mentioned. If some of the salespeople are the type who must leave the room to brighten it, the best way to turn them around at the start of a meeting is with a powerful opening inspiration.

Most people are not intentionally negative; it is simply that they would rather be somewhere else trying to grow their business. If their minds are preoccupied, a strong opening inspiration is a positive way to get everyone on the same page. Since sales is a difficult job, many people appreciate various types of positive inspirations. You can find these quotes, stories, poems, or articles in many places: throughout this book, on our website at www.nextlevelsales consulting.com, or in other books and publications. Here's one example:

What Am I?

I will push you onward or drag you down to failure. I am completely at your command. Half the things you do you might just as well turn over to me and I will be able to do them quickly and correctly.

I am easily managed—you must merely be firm with me. Show me exactly how you want something done; and after a few lessons, I will do it automatically. I am the servant of all great men; and alas, of all failures as well. Those who are great, I have made great. Those who are failures, I have made failures.

I am not a machine, though I work with all the precision of a machine plus the intelligence of a man. You may run me for a profit or run me for ruin—it makes no difference to me.

Take me, train me, be firm with me and I will place the world at your feet. Be easy with me and I will destroy you. You know by now, my friend, that I am your habits.

If your meeting started at 8:00, it's now 8:02, and the tone has been all positive so far. The coach or a team member has read or recited the opening inspiration and everyone is feeling positive and running on a rainbow.

Success Stories

In the days of ancient Rome, when gladiators used to fight one another, there was one particularly strong gladiator named Androcles. Androcles easily made handiwork out of every human opponent that came his way. So after he had defeated all worthy men, the people of Rome arranged a final battle between Androcles and a lion. The battle began in front of a packed Coliseum, and right away the lion leaped at Androcles. Androcles swiftly dodged the lion and ended up behind it. From that position, Androcles leaned over and whispered into the lion's ear and immediately the lion turned over on its back with all four paws in the air to give up and forfeit victory to Androcles. Caesar, who was sitting in the Coliseum, was amazed by what he saw, so he arranged for one of his guards to bring Androcles to him. Caesar congratulated Androcles and then asked how he beat the lion so easily: "Androcles, what did you say to the lion?" Androcles responded, "I told the lion, listen lion, you realize if you beat me, all fifty thousand of these people are going to want to know how you did it. You're going to have to give a 15-minute impromptu speech on the strategies and tactics you used to defeat me."

Like the lion, many people would prefer not to speak in public. In fact, according to The Book of Lists, the 10 worst human fears in the U.S. are, in order from most to least dreaded:

1. Speaking before a group
2. Heights
3. Insects and bugs
4. Financial problems
5. Deep water
6. Sickness
7. Death
8. Flying
9. Loneliness
10. Dogs

As comedian Jerry Seinfeld points out, "That means if you're at a funeral, you'd rather be in the casket than delivering the eulogy."

Success stories, which are easy subjects to talk about, can be used both as a means to overcoming this fear of speaking and as a way to share best practices.

Sharing success stories is also an excellent way to continue the positive momentum after the opening inspiration. At this point in the meeting, the most successful teams have each person stand up one at a time to share a personal win since the last meeting. In a sales meeting it is important to get people on their feet as much as possible. This helps them stay engaged. Other benefits of standing up to present success stories early in the meeting include:

- The meeting becomes interactive right away, so the amount of positive energy in the room stays strong.
- Salespeople are recognized by their coach and their peers for their great efforts and outstanding results.
- Best practices are shared, which helps improve everyone's results.
- Salespeople build credibility when they describe their experiences to the team.
- Salespeople build confidence in their ability to speak to groups when they present to the team.

In general, people like sharing good news. Here are a few things to keep in mind to make this portion of the meeting run smoothly:

- Have people prepare success stories in advance of the meeting so that they are prepared with their biggest wins and so that they can be succinct. The preparation is simple when you make this the start of each meeting.
- If the coach or a salesperson would like a certain salesperson to share a specific story, be sure to tell that person in advance.
- Limit each success story to one minute.
- The coach should share a success story first to set the positive tone and demonstrate how to tell a succinct story and stay within the time limit.

- The coach and salespeople can give quick feedback and recognition after individuals share.
- Applaud after each story as an extra form of recognition and to keep the energy up in the meeting.

Here are a few examples of what success stories may sound like:

Joel: I have been so persistent prospecting Ian's Corndog Café. I have called them at least 30 times, and I can never get past Cecilia, the gatekeeper, to speak with Ian himself, who makes all the decisions. So finally I came in early Thursday, called at 5:30 A.M., and got in touch with Ian. I made an appointment to meet with him this afternoon. This could be a big deal!

Leigh: I had an initial meeting with that big law firm, Dewey, Cheatam, and Howe. All three key decision makers attended: Jennine, Bob, and Ava. They are very qualified and seem really excited about a long-term commitment. My presentation meeting is on Friday and Mindy is coming with me to help close the deal!

Scotty: I just got the signed proposal yesterday from Raleigh's Restaurant. They should be a great client. They've already signed on for a year. And, with that sale, I've exceeded my quota for the quarter!

If you introduce sharing success stories to your sales meetings and it is a new concept, it may be a bit uncomfortable for some, especially when people have to stand up. Do it anyway! My mentor always asks me if I would rather be comfortable with my current level of success or uncomfortable and more successful. The major obstacles that a coach or a team face during this portion of the meeting are, first, people who do not want to stand, and second, people who have nothing positive to share.

It is the coach's responsibility to address the first challenge. The coach must stand to tell his success story. Then the coach must choose another enthusiastic, positive team member to go second. This person will also not resist standing. So the team starts a pattern of standing and it soon becomes the standard way that people present their success stories. To address the second challenge of people with no good news, the coach must pre-empt this problem. If a coach is doing a great job of conducting GSMs, following up, and coaching in the crunch, he should be familiar with some successes from each salesperson before the meeting even starts. Then if someone has nothing to say, the coach can remind that person of something positive and have her share that story. If this becomes a regular occurrence with the same person, the coach can approach the salesperson prior to the meeting and tell her what to share. Very soon, that salesperson will get the point.

Now you are a few minutes into the meeting. You are all inspired, everyone has shared a recent success, and the entire team is grinning so wide they could eat bananas sideways.

Training

Before actually eating the bananas, we suggest you incorporate a team training session in your sales meetings, as the top sales teams do. You can follow the same training process outlined in detail in Chapter 5. Here it is again for you. See Figure 7.2.

In a team setting the coach or team should select a training topic that addresses a skill gap that is common among the team members. For example, the team may practice delivering their value propositions, asking for referrals, or making cold calls. We've found it is important, though, not to try to cover eight skills within one team training session. You have a limited amount of time, so pick one or maybe two related areas and practice them properly.

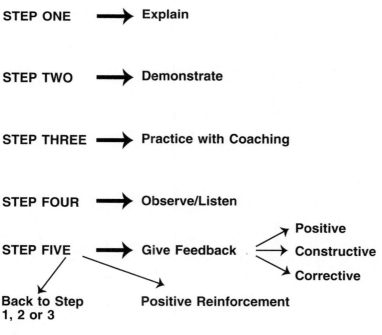

FIGURE 7.2 The Training Process

When we say properly, here's what we mean. The training leader (most often the coach) will give a quick skill explanation and demonstration. As always, higher caliber demonstrations yield higher caliber results from team members. When salespeople are practicing skills, make sure they stand on their feet. This further engages all the participants and keeps the vibe upbeat. Everyone should be practicing at the same time, in pairs or trios, switching partners after each iteration. The leader can use a bell and/or stopwatch to keep the team structured. This approach may sound a bit militant, but the best sales teams use these tools, and salespeople start to appreciate all this practice when they realize they are improving. This practice with coaching step is where repetition comes into play. It is an area in which the great teams and coaches stand out from the good ones. Good teams practice how to resolve an objection or how to set an agenda or whichever skill is most relevant, for two to three iterations, and move on. Great teams practice the same skills, but for six to eight iterations or more, until everyone on the team feels like they can't wait to run out of the meeting and execute on a real live prospect or client. This may seem boring or overly repetitive, but it's what the great teams do, so great coaches must have an uniquely high tolerance for repetition. Great teams also will include a portion of the training, after several rounds of practice, in which each team member will stand on his feet and deliver the skill to the group. This is a fine opportunity for recognition and helps encourage salespeople to take the practice sessions seriously.

Now we are halfway through the meeting and each person is feeling good, is participating, and has learned and practiced useful skills.

Scoreboard—Goal Reporting and Setting

"There must be a mechanism that measures how we're doing and it must always be there."

> —John Swenson, sales executive,
> Avnet, a semiconductor
> distributor

One of our favorite clients at The Next Level is the Los Angeles Clippers NBA basketball team. We do not work with the players, but we do work with their sales team and sales coaches. To support our clients and because we love the team, we are season ticket holders and attend many of the games each season. In the center of the Staples Center arena, where the Clippers play, hangs a large scoreboard so everyone in the arena can see it. Why is it visible to everyone? Because it has an impact on everyone there: players, coaches, and fans. When a player makes a basket, the scoreboard changes. The players become motivated by the score change. Then the fans cheer or boo. The fans' cheers and boos impact the players' performance and encourage them to play harder. The coach sees the score change on the scoreboard, and he makes coaching decisions accordingly. These decisions ideally help the players perform at an even higher level, so the scoreboard lights up again.

A public scoreboard is just as important in a sales culture as it is at a basketball game. To carry forth our analogy, the players on the court are like the salesperson that has his turn to score with sales activity and results. When a salesperson sees his numbers on the board versus those of his peers, he is typically motivated, just like the players in the game. The fans at the game are analogous to all the other salespeople at the meeting. When one person puts his numbers on the board, the team members will either cheer with praise or respond less positively if the numbers are not great, in the same way that the fans boo. (Incidentally, we do not encourage booing at your sales meeting.) The coach on the court, of course, plays the same role as the sales coach in the meeting. As she looks at the results on the scoreboard, she strategizes and plans tactics for the entire team as well as for individual participants.

Let's look at the example of a scoreboard shown in Figure 7.3 and walk through a scenario of how this may work. Keep in mind that you can customize your team's scoreboard to be as specific or as general as you'd like.

At this point in the meeting it is time for each team member to update the weekly scoreboard. One at a time, each salesperson takes a marker and writes his results from last week or month and sets goals for the subsequent period. If Gene St. Pierre is first up, he limps slowly up to the board and records his numbers. It's pretty clear that Gene had a rough week. Then he writes down his goals for the next week, which should be somewhat in sync with the goals set in his GSM. The point is not to humiliate anyone; it's merely to inspire great performance. As Gene walks back to his seat in the meeting there will probably not be too many fans cheering, and the coach may make note of a discussion that should happen after the meeting in follow-up or at an upcoming GSM. This is a bit uncomfortable for Gene, but it is a necessary part of good sales coaching. If Gene is in it to win it, he should feel a fire in his belly to improve so that he does not have the same experience at the next sales meeting.

It's Mark Freeark's turn next. Mark struts up to the scoreboard with his shoulders high and his chest out. He had a great week. He

Team Johnson Scoreboard

Name		Last Goal	Actual	+/-	Next Goal
St Pierre	Appointments Set	5	2	−3	6
	Appointment Held	4	1	−3	4
	New Accounts	1	0	−1	2
Freeark	Appointments Set	5	6	+1	5
	Appointment Held	4	5	+1	4
	New Accounts	1	2	+1	2
Sullivan	Appointments Set				
	Appointment Held				
	New Accounts				
Baiada	Appointments Set				
	Appointment Held				
	New Accounts				
Walker	Appointments Set				
	Appointment Held				
	New Accounts				
Dunlay	Appointments Set				
	Appointment Held				
	New Accounts				
Kolesar	Appointments Set				
	Appointment Held				
	New Accounts				
Lopez	Appointments Set				
	Appointment Held				
	New Accounts				
Fontenette	Appointments Set				
	Appointment Held				
	New Accounts				
Scarcello	Appointments Set				
	Appointment Held				
	New Accounts				
Tapia	Appointments Set				
	Appointment Held				
	New Accounts				

FIGURE 7.3 Team Johnson Scoreboard

not only hit but exceeded his goal in each key performance indicator. Mark then sets big goals for next week too, hoping to close two more accounts. Mark should get a tremendously positive response from the "fans" and coach that recognize his great week and admire his confidence with the big goals he wrote down for next week.

These are two extreme examples, positive and negative, and your team members will be all over the board at times. Our clients have come up with names for this portion of the meeting referring to the team's response to either great or not so great performance. There's the walk of fame, or the walk of shame; cheers or jeers; thumbs up or thumbs down.

When the scoreboard lights up, just as in a basketball game, salespeople receive immediate feedback from the coach and their peers. This recognition is huge. Let's look at how this impacts salespeople at each level.

The top 20 percent of your sales team likes being in the top spot and wants to stay there. They love the time each week when they get to put their big numbers on the board and shine in front of the team. These people may be the future leaders of your organization, they lead by example, and they deserve the positive recognition.

The big middle 60 percent also gets motivated by results reporting on the scoreboard. Most of this group become inspired by the performance of the top 20 percent, and they aspire to copy the top performers' aggressive goals and best practices, so they too can be at that level soon.

The bottom 20 percent should also get fired up! This positive peer pressure should help them quickly figure out whether they are going to move up or out. They must adjust their habits to create stronger performance or start working on their resumes.

All of this is very healthy. Coaches ask us all the time how to motivate their weakest performers to change. This scoreboarding practice is one of the most effective ways we have seen top sales coaches pull out the weeds on their teams. The best performers receive the recognition they deserve. Johnny Hardluck and Sally Badnews, who consistently under perform, will eventually weed themselves out, because no one likes having this experience every week or every month.

Great coaches and teams apply these techniques because scoreboarding publicly encourages the top performers to stay at the top, the middle performers to move up, and discourages poor performance altogether.

Summary and Action Items

The meeting is almost over! This next step is not rocket science, but it is important. You have positive momentum, everyone has been through training, and people are motivated by the scoreboard; now it's time to bring this baby down for a smooth landing. Someone should be taking notes throughout the meeting. Many teams rotate this responsibility. At this point, the secretary can quickly summarize all of the key points from the meeting, paying special attention to review all of the important action items and who is responsible for following up on each one. The secretary should then send out the notes or minutes to the rest of the team after the meeting. Again, this is not too complicated, just a quick and clean way to tie up loose ends.

Next Meeting Logistics and Assignment

This step is simple but important. Before the closing inspiration, confirm the date and time of the next meeting or the next few meetings. Then make sure everyone is clear on the assignments that must be completed for the next meeting. For example, salespeople may need to bring with them a certain script for the training exercise next time, or, in our meetings at The Next Level, we all read a book and give a quick oral report at the next meeting. Also, when you get to the stage in which different team members are leading different parts of the sales meeting (we are about to discuss that), here is where you confirm who is doing what.

Closing Inspiration

End the meeting with a bang, just like the way you started it! People should come out of a sales meeting feeling positive, but this doesn't always happen. The following is an example of an ineffective meeting that does not leave teammates feeling positive. (SRJ) I remember an old basketball coach I had. In one particular game, late in the fourth quarter my team was getting killed. For all intents and purposes, the game was over, and playing the last few minutes was a formality. Coach called us over to huddle and his speech went something like this: "You guys stink. You're not playing hard at all. OK. Put your hands in. Hustle on 3. 1-2-3-Hustle!" And we went back out onto the court feeling worse than we did before the huddle. Sales meetings should leave people feeling just the opposite, ready to conquer their goals in the week or month ahead. Here are two examples of closing inspirations you can share with your team.

It is not the critic who counts, nor the man who points out how the strong man stumbled, or where the doer of deeds could have done them better. The credit belongs to the man who is actually in the arena, whose face is marred by dust and sweat and blood; who strives valiantly, who errs and comes up short again and again; who knows the great enthusiasms, the great devotions, and spends himself in a worthy cause; who at the best knows in the end the triumphs of high achievement and who at the worst if he fails, at least fails while daring greatly, so that his place shall never be with those cold and timid souls who know neither defeat nor victory.

—Theodore Roosevelt

The clock is running. Make the most of today. To realize the value of one year, ask a student who failed a grade. To realize the value of one month, ask the mother who gave birth to a premature baby. To realize the value of one week, ask the editor of a weekly newspaper. To realize the value of one hour, ask the lovers who are waiting to meet. To realize the value of one minute, ask a person who missed the train. To realize the value of one second, ask a person who just avoided an accident. To realize the value of one millisecond, ask the person who won a silver medal in the Olympics.

—*The Executive Speechwriter Newsletter*

Getting Others Involved

A very wealthy man bought a huge ranch in Arizona and invited some of his closer associates to see it. After touring the 1,500 acres of mountains, rivers, and grasslands, he took everybody to the house. The house was as spectacular as the scenery. In the back of the house was the largest swimming pool they had ever seen.

However, it was filled with alligators. The owner explained: "I value courage more than anything. It is what made me a billionaire. I value courage so much that if anyone has the courage to jump in that pool and swim to the other side, I will give them whatever they want, my land, my house, my money, anything."

Of course, everybody laughed at the challenge and turned to follow the owner into the house for lunch. Suddenly they heard a splash. Turning around they saw a guy splashing and thrashing in the water, swimming for his life as the alligators swarmed after him. After several death-defying seconds, the man made it unharmed to the other side. The billionaire was amazed but he stuck to his promise. He said, "You are a man of courage, you can have any thing you want, the house, my money, my land, etc., whatever you want is yours." The swimmer, breathing heavily, looked up and said, "I just want to know who pushed me in the pool."

Some people do need a little push to get involved and the more that people are involved in a sales meeting, the better. The quality of the meeting is directly related to the quality of the participation in the meeting. Once the coach and the team become very comfortable with the format of these sales meetings, after many weeks or months, the coach can begin to have salespeople take part in facilitating portions of the meeting. This is a great way to encourage your organization's future leaders to step up and start leading by coaching their peers. When salespeople effectively lead portions of the meeting, the energy can really be great, because generally people will want to see their peers succeed, especially if they know they will be on their feet in front of the group soon.

The way this works is that the coach simply chooses certain salespeople to lead certain parts of the meeting. Some coaches delegate roles at each meeting for the subsequent meeting. You may use a template like the one shown in Figure 7.4.

The choice of who does what cannot just be a random assignment from the coach. If this happens, the meeting can turn to chaos, and people will not be interested in leading again. The coach should delegate carefully and strategically, one portion at a time, beginning with the top performers. Then it is the coach's job to

---

Next Meeting's Assignments

Agenda Item	Facilitator	Time
Opening Inspiration		2 Min.
Success Stories		1 Min./Person
Training		25 Min.
• Topic		
Scoreboard	Coach	10 Min.
Summary and action Items		5 Min.
Next Meeting Logistics and Assignments	Coach	2 Min.
Closing Inspiration		1 Min.

FIGURE 7.4   Next Meeting's Assignments

make sure each person is ready to lead her portion effectively. For example, if a coach is going to have the top salesperson lead training on resolving objections for the next meeting's training, the coach should schedule time, in advance of the sales meeting, one-on-one with the top performer to review the handouts and go through a dry run of the training presentation.

Sales Huddles

Sales huddles are simply a quicker, and often more regular, version of a sales meeting. Some of our clients in financial services gather all the salespeople and coaches together every morning for 10 to 15 minutes to set the tone and explain the specific sales focus for the day. Many of our clients who work in a call center sales environment have a great deal of success with short, daily huddles to share wins, review new information, and motivate the team. In a widely spread outside sales team, daily huddles can happen over a conference call.

The 2001 NFL Champion Baltimore Ravens football team is a great example of a team that utilized brief huddles to focus and motivate team members. On offense, quarterback Trent Dilfer led the huddles, and on defense, it was linebacker Ray Lewis. The huddle leader brings all the players together to prepare them for battle before the next play. They establish a focus and everyone is on the same page. There's also a lot of encouragement and recognition that happens in a football team's huddle, and it is no different in a sales huddle. Some football teams even hold hands in their huddles as a sign of team. You can do that with your sales team, but you may want to run it by your HR department first.

On sales teams, many coaches prepare the night before for the next day's huddle, or some do so early each morning. The best coaches, who run huddles, make the quick preparation part of their regular routine. This preparation is key, because with only 10 to 15 minutes, the coach must be able to focus and motivate the team in a very short period of time. It's his or her only chance to deliver a clear message to the entire team.

Here's an example of a sales huddle agenda:

- Opening inspiration.
- Yesterday's results vs. goals.
- Share 1–2 success stories.
- Share 1–2 challenges and potential solutions.
- Set the focus or goals for the day ahead (e.g. new product, promotion, or sales incentive).
- Closing inspiration.

Other Best Practices on Meetings/Huddles from Top Sales Teams

- Some sales organizations cover operational issues in separate meetings to keep the sales meeting focused on sales.
- Some sales organizations have meetings on Friday afternoons and reward strong performance with the rest of the day off. Poor performance means more sales activity on Friday afternoon.
- Giving pre-work and small assignments before sales meetings improves the quality of the skill development/training time.
- Daily huddles are a great forum for setting daily goals. This helps the entire team focus on the right behaviors.

- Daily huddles must last 15 minutes or less.
- The scoreboard should be in a place in the office that is visible all the time, by everyone in all functions, sales and others. Some teams use it as the wallpaper on their computer and update it each day.
- A great time to do follow-up is right after your meeting or huddle.

Your meeting or your huddle is over. If you are a coach, it is now time to get to work following up, conducting GSMs, coaching in the crunch, or leading individual training sessions. Go out and catch people doing the right things. If you are a salesperson, you have just heard an uplifting closing inspiration and you are ready to go out and dominate the world, or at least your sales territory.

In Chapter 8 we will round out our coaching puzzle with an important section on recognition. Sales activities and coaching activities are great, and everyone is happier when these activities occur within a positive sales culture fueled by coach and peer recognition.

8 Recognition

"ADP has always prided itself on recognition. So whether we are running a meeting with 8 people, 80 people, or 400 people—there must be recognition at the beginning, middle, and end of that meeting. And it's as important to recognize personal achievements like weddings, as it is professional achievements."
—Mark Benjamin, Vice President
of National Sales at Automatic Data
Processing (ADP) TotalSource

(SRJ) At the end of my first year in sales I was 23 years old and I made the 250 Club. I had achieved $250,000 in sales, and I was on top of the world. I got to walk across the stage at the auditorium where the annual awards ceremony was held, and shake the president of the company's hand. We took a picture and the president handed me a bonus check for $1,500. There were 1,000 other salespeople in the audience looking on that day, and every one of them saw me enter the 250 Club—Boo ya! The best part about this experience is what it did for me. I really tasted success for the first time. I liked it, I loved it, and I wanted some more of it! The experience made me want to become even more committed and take my sales success to an even higher level. Next year I wanted to make the 375 Club. I did. In fact, I was up on that stage accepting an award ten years in a row. It never got tired or boring. It was fun every time, and each time it helped me sustain my momentum into the next year.

As this example illustrates, effective recognition can propel salespeople to even higher levels of performance. If you think back to the time in your career when you really made great strides and broke through, your success was probably recognized by and shared with peers and/or coaches. On the other hand, when salespeople reach a milestone or accomplishment and it goes unnoticed, they are not as motivated to continue to move forward.

Before we discuss recognition further and offer several examples of how it has been used effectively, we need to make one important point. Recognition does not replace coaching or any of the other pieces of the model presented throughout this book. (See Figure 8.1.) In fact, the leader of the sales team can be the king or queen of recognition, but if all of the other coaching elements are not in place, the team will be unlikely to reach its potential over the long haul. The steps of the coaching model (Planning, GSMs, Training, Follow up, Coaching in the Crunch and Sales Meetings) are the cake. Using recognition effectively is the icing. Used properly, recognition can grease the skids for each of the components of the coaching model, enabling coaches and salespeople to become even more successful.

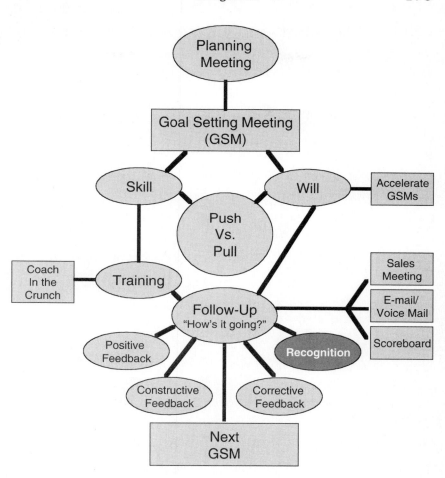

FIGURE 8.1 Coaching Model 8

There are entire books written about recognition, incentives, and sales contests, with more ideas on implementing these programs than you could ever imagine. There are yearly plans with cash bonuses and incentive trips, as well as quarterly, monthly, weekly, even daily selling contests. People are recognized with plaques, titles, certificates, prizes, or with advanced training programs. We will not attempt to outline all of the various methods of providing recognition. Instead we will share some of the more effective approaches to recognition that we have observed. By "effective" with recognition we mean that all these examples have driven the right behaviors in salespeople and motivated those who achieve to reach even higher ground, and motivated those who didn't achieve not to miss the target next time.

A Recognition Paradigm

John Maly, who runs a 700-employee company and oversees a several hundred person sales force in the beauty product distribution business, recently described how he perceives recognition with a simple analogy. John explained an instance in which his 12-year-old son, Austin, babysat for a couple of hours for Austin's younger brother, Luke. When John spoke to Austin about how he had done, he recognized Austin's efforts and praised him for being "so responsible." John did this because he loves Austin and was proud of him, not because he wanted Austin to do anything. Now, maybe Austin will be more willing to help with babysitting next time, and maybe he will even look forward to the next opportunity, but these benefits are simply outgrowths of John's recognition. His intent in recognition was simply to praise his son because he was proud of his accomplishment and because he cares about him.

John explains how he thinks about recognizing his employees in the same way: "Just like I'm happy for a friend when he succeeds, I recognize my people because I care about them, and I am proud of them." Outgrowths of that recognition may be that people stay motivated, sell even more, or stay at Maly's company longer, but that is not John's primary intent in providing recognition. For example, John has recently introduced an executive incentive program to reward his employees. Recently someone asked him if that was a retention tool. John replied that the additional incentive program is not for retention, it is because he wants to say thank you. This is pretty genuine and comes from the same guy who sends 700 birthday cards each year (one to each employee) with a personal handwritten note in each one.

Little Things are Big

Dave Doehr, a sales executive with a large telecom company, believes strongly that, "you can never underestimate the power of simple recognition for a job well done." Dave uses a very simple (and cheap) system of giving handwritten notes to the people on his team every time one goes above and beyond. During a time when Dave's team was focused on selling DSL products, Dave created a "DSL Warrior" card, on which he would write the notes. He explains: "People would hang the warriors all over their work areas, and each time they looked at them, they were reminded to go the extra mile for one of our customers." Writing the notes takes time, but Dave believes it is worth every second, for the end result he achieves: a motivated team that thrives on recognition.

A training director at a financial services firm gave us another example of how little things can make a big difference when it comes to recognition. At this firm, each monthly training class has between 100 and 150 members. The training director was speaking to the top salesperson in a particular class regarding a technical glitch in the ranking system that showed how each member of the training class was performing relative to the others. The director explained that everything was fine and that, despite the glitch, the salesperson's production numbers and compensation would be handled properly. The salesperson made it very clear that correcting the production numbers for the sake of his compensation was not what he was concerned about. Jokingly, he announced: "I know I'll get paid. I just want you to fix the reporting system so the number two salesperson will see just how far behind me he is." Putting someone's name in lights in this way is a very inexpensive way to keep top performers motivated.

Lastly, regarding the little things, as Doug Neet, a sales executive at New York Life, puts it, "Anybody can buy a plaque for $15, but it's what's on the plaque that matters. It's a symbol of your effort, and we all want praise for our effort."

Voice Mail and E-Mail

"When I was a salesperson, recognition was huge to me. I was told not to ever forget what it was like to be in the field, in the trenches."

—Carla Savko, sales coach,
Maly's beauty product distributor

Each morning before 7 A.M. Carla sends a voice mail with high-lights from the day before. She mentions everyone on the team that sold above a certain number yesterday and she shares success sto-ries. Her people love it and tell her that her message gets them out of the funk in the morning if they're not feeling positive. Then team members send general voice mails to the rest of the team rec-ognizing one another's performance, so peers are pushing one an-other in the right direction. Carla says this really helps keep people inspired because, "Let's face it, when it is one hundred degrees out-side and it's your twelfth call of the day, you can use a little extra motivation."

While her voice mails to the salespeople, and the subsequent voice mails between salespeople, are very personal techniques to provide recognition, Carla also very effectively uses e-mail to rec-ognize team and individual strong performance. Figure 8.2 shows an e-mail in which she uses pictures and a sound bite that are aligned with her company's Goal Achiever's Trip to Mexico. This approach obviously makes the top salespeople feel great and moti-vates the others to step up. She also clearly posts sales results (score-boarding) in the e-mail and thanks her salespeople: a very effective form of recognition.

A Family Affair

Mark Benjamin at ADP described a particularly effective sales con-test in which the winners received flat screen TVs. One smart tactic the company used to execute the contest involved sales manage-ment teams sending material promoting the contest to all of the

June Actual Results!

◀﹚ Click to play sound: Taxiing Jet

Cabo San Lucas Here we come!!

Record Breakers.....

Best day ever $67,000
Best month ever $530,730 (history of all Team Maly's)
9 DSCs best month ever!!!!
9 DSCs hit budget!!
2 DSCs over $70,000 (Gina and Don)
Every DSC over $40,000
19.2% over budget!!
31 Paul Mitchell 693.00 deals!

Tammy	59,878
Monique	49,297
Sara	48,990
Sally	41,654
Robert	52,103
Quinn	43,113
Don	70,760
Gina	70,308
Lori	45,624
Randy	49,005

At this rate we will all be going to Cabo San Lucas!!!! Margaritas, Olé!!!

Keep up the great focus!! Again Many Thanks for all you do ***EVERY DAY!!***

Gracias!!! Adios!!!

FIGURE 8.2   Cabo San Lucas

salespeople's homes. As Mark put it, "Each salesperson's entire family was pulling for success. Our salespeople's kids were excited that 'Mommy or Daddy can win a flat screen!' " This particular contest was very successful at ADP and a significant portion of the sales force won a TV. While some contests have salespeople or sales teams competing against each other, this one required a certain individual level of sales performance over a few months. All the salespeople in the company could have won if they each had achieved the hurdles.

Dress the Part

We asked our humble haberdasher, Holli Bhaskar, a sales coach and salesperson with Tom James Company, for his unique perspective. Holli sells custom-fit clothing and has been treated to several President's Club incentive trips for him and his wife after exceeding his own sales quota. Interestingly, many sales organizations use Holli's products and services as incentives. Sony presented its top salespeople with a Samurai Award in which the top achievers won a head-to-toe, custom-made wardrobe. To emphasize the recognition of the top performers, the sales leadership actually had Holli come up onto the award stage and take the measurements of the award winners in front of the rest of the sales team. This gave the top people a little extra time to bask in the glory of success.

Healthy Competition

In many of the sales organizations we work with, it seems that the best sales performers are fueled even more by some healthy competition. Recently we spoke with a manager and salesperson at a financial services firm, who described his scenario at the firm when he started seven years ago in a training class of 235 salespeople. He and a friend from the training class recognized great potential in one another, and they agreed to stay in touch and closely track one another's performance to foster some healthy competition, even though one lived in Phoenix and the other in Kansas City. Seven years later, they are two of the only three members of their training class of 235 still employed at the firm. He does not think it's a coincidence and neither do we. Having peers help with accountability in a friendly yet competitive way is a common thread among top salespeople, especially those who do not have a regular coach working with them.

Another way healthy competition can stimulate sales results is within a team setting. Dave Conti, Director of Sales at Enterprise Fleet Services, a division of Enterprise Rent-A-Car, explains, "We have sales contests in which we pit branch versus branch, and we include everyone—managers, salespeople, and administrative people. That way everyone feels accountable to everyone else, and there's more momentum toward the prize. It's the difference between a salesperson asking an administrative person to stay late to work on a proposal 'because I have a contest deadline' versus because 'we have a contest deadline.'" Mike Mejia, Vice President of Sales at Adelphia, uses the same strategy, "We include every employee in our sales contests—from sales to tracking to administrative. Everyone becomes more motivated and focused on the company's goals. This way we motivate not only the people that bring in business, but also the people that hold the business together."

Other Tips with Recognition

- "Make sure you don't go backwards," says Nitya Kirat, a friend who works in pharmaceutical sales. When planning sales incentives and contests, try to think as long-term as possible. The contests should get better and better or at least stay on the same level. If the prize goes from big to not as big, salespeople will not be as excited and the program can have adverse effects.

- Contests, bonus systems, and other programs are never perfectly fair for everyone. Someone will always complain about how he or she is at a disadvantage. Life is not fair. Make the best of the situation you are in.

- When setting benchmarks as targets, do not print and advertise minimums. If you do, that is what you'll get—minimal performance. Having a goal and a stretch goal tends to be a more effective strategy.

- Titles are an amazing way to give free recognition. A manager in financial services comments, "When financial advisors hit a certain production level, we give them a bigger title. Even though it means nothing, they get a huge confidence boost out of it."

- "The investment in contests is small potatoes compared to the reward we receive in incremental revenue, and I can easily sell these projects internally because they are always self-funding."–Bob DeTrano, sales executive, Starwood Hotels.

- According to Dave Doehr, a sales executive in telecom, "If a compensation structure sends a signal to the people at the bottom that it may be time to leave, it is an effective program."

- According to Mark Benjamin at ADP, "the benchmark is set right for a contest or incentive trip if about 30 to 50 percent make it. The top 3 to 5 percent will be there anyway. These rewards are in place to get the next larger group to the next level. You can still do something nice for the top 5 percent, like a special cocktail hour with the CEO or upgraded hotel rooms, and that does what you need in giving them the extra bit of recognition."

- Loren Ahlgren, Vice President of Fleet Services at Enterprise Rent-A-Car, points out the value of regular incentive programs, "We have contests monthly, and some branches do them weekly so there's always something to look forward to."

- If you are a salesperson who does not work closely with a coach or a team, you can still recognize yourself. It is great to share your sales victories with friends and family. Also, when you do self-GSMs and hit your goals, treat yourself to something nice. Buy that new pair of shoes, or new car, or take that vacation you have earned. Keep yourself motivated with incentives.

Summary

We have reviewed several unique methods that can be implemented to highlight and recognize strong performance. The bottom line is that, to ensure continued success among salespeople, it is important to make a big deal out of it when people succeed, and to let others know about it. The person being recognized will feel confident, motivated, and on top of the world, and everyone around him will become motivated so that they can experience that feeling as well. Remember, though, all this recognition is not a substitute for strong coaching. It is simply rocket fuel for the coach instead of regular old 87 octane, so it takes coaching to a whole new level.

9 | Tying It All Together

Congratulations! You are finished! You now know what it takes to create a great salesperson within yourself or in someone else. We all know that is important because *Selling is Everyone's Business*! When you are in a position in which you need to wield influence on others (and we all are, almost every day), you become a salesperson. And everyone who is a salesperson, either in their career or in situations where they need to influence others, can benefit from a coach, whether you are your own coach, you have a coach, or you are a coach for others. As you move on in your career, remember the following:

- A coach succeeds by helping others succeed. A boss commands and demands.
- Coaching takes a conscious effort. It is not easy and it requires a great deal of time and energy. And it's worth it.

- Your business plan serves as your compass for salesperson and coach that can guide your monthly, weekly, and daily plans and actions.
- A goal-setting meeting is a consistent, scheduled one-on-one meeting between salesperson and coach in which the duo reviews performance from the previous period and creates and commits to a game plan and short-term action steps for the upcoming period. GSMs are a fundamental piece to the coaching puzzle.
- Within a GSM, remember the following steps:

  1. *Present the Agenda:* A clear focus is established and the group is in agreement on the meeting contents.
  2. *Discovery:* The coach asks questions to understand what worked and what did not work and to gather information to create the next period's plan.
  3. *Solution and Game Plan:* The pair works together to create SMART goals and action steps for both salesperson and coach.
  4. *Summary and Commitment:* Both parties recap and confirm responsibilities and deadlines.
  5. *Encouragement:* A closing statement that leaves people feeling motivated and inspired.

- Use the following training process to address individual and team skill issues:

  1. *Explain* the skill.
  2. *Demonstrate* the skill at a high level from the coach.
  3. *Practice with Coaching* repeating several times to build confidence.

4. *Observe* each other to create coachable moments.
5. *Give Feedback* to improve performance with positive, constructive, and corrective advice.

- Coaches must follow up spontaneously with their people by asking 'How's it going?' Then follow that question with "What's working" and "What's not working?"
- During follow-up, coaches will identify skill and will issues and can deliver more positive, constructive, and corrective feedback.
- When coaching in the crunch, the coach should transition from leader to supporter to observer, taking less and less control of the call each time.
- Top sales organizations use a standardized evaluation tool while coaching in the crunch to document progress and give meaningful feedback.
- The suggested sales meeting agenda includes the following steps:

  1. Opening inspiration.
  2. Success stories.
  3. Training.
  4. Scoreboard—Goal reporting and setting.
  5. Summary and action items.
  6. Next meeting logistics and assignment.
  7. Closing inspiration.

- Encourage meeting participation and interactivity to get people out of their comfort zones.
- Many teams have success with sales huddles, which are simply quicker and more regular versions of sales meetings.

- The purpose of recognition is to make people feel great about the work they've done and to thank them. Recognition does not replace coaching, it augments coaching.

It's critical to realize that each of these coaching facets works to support each other. Embracing one or two will help, but it is the coordinated effort of yearly business plans, regularly scheduled GSMs, consistent training, constant follow-up, regular coaching in the crunch, dynamic sales meetings, and proper recognition that will truly create the perfect salesperson.

Go ahead and get started—schedule a business planning meeting or a GSM. Get ready to improve your personal and professional lives and get ready to make everyone else around you better too!

Index

Page numbers in italics indicate a figure.

What We Do and How to Contact Us

At The Next Level, we work with numerous high-profile clients including Automatic Data Processing (ADP), A.G. Edwards & Sons Inc., Adelphia, Bank of America, Countrywide Financial, Enterprise Rent-A-Car, IndyMac Bank, the Los Angeles Clippers, Maly's, Morgan Stanley, Piper Jaffray, RBC Dain Rauscher, UBS Financial Services, and Vanguard. For these wide-ranging clients we perform a variety of functions including determining best practices, designing sales/service improvement programs, facilitating instructor-led training, implementing follow-up plans with sales executives and sales coaches, keeping score of results to track a return on investment, and delivering keynote speeches.

Example project goals include:

- Increase sales and profitability.
- Transition a service organization to a sales organization.
- Improve coaching, accountability, and follow-up skills of sales executives and sales managers.
- Transfer best practices to everyone on the team.
- Increase business with existing customers.
- Improve employee morale and retention.
- Improve productivity per salesperson.
- Shorten the sales cycle.
- Improve conversion rate over the phone or face-to-face.

Each of these initiatives is achieved through a customized program based on company, industry, and cross-industry relevant best coaching and sales practices.

If your sales organization is looking to take its performance to the next level, please contact us at:

The Next Level Sales Consulting
2321 Rosecrans Ave., Suite 4250
El Segundo, CA 90245
www.nextlevelsalesconsulting.com

Steve Johnson
stevej@nextlevelsalesconsulting.com
(310) 643-7700

Adam Shaivitz
adams@nextlevelsalesconsulting.com
or
ashaivitz@yahoo.com
(310) 643-7700
(310) 502-4315 (c)